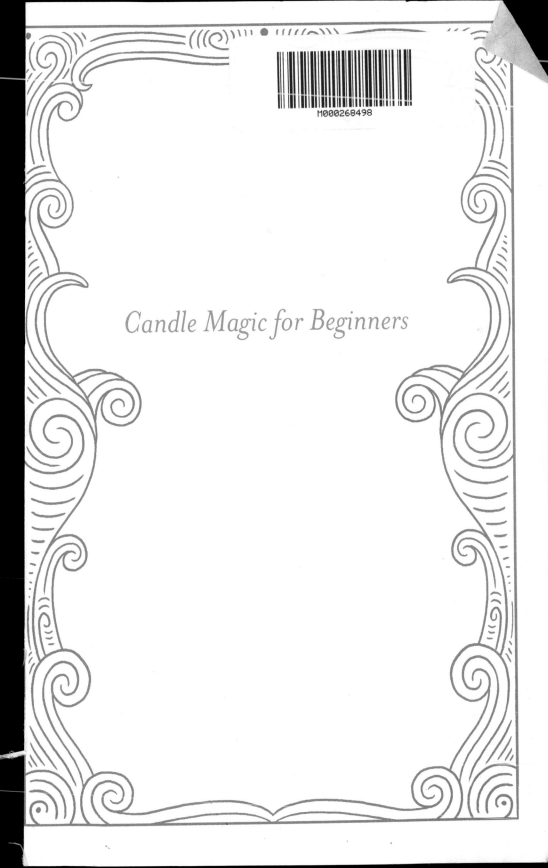

*Candle Magic for Beginners*

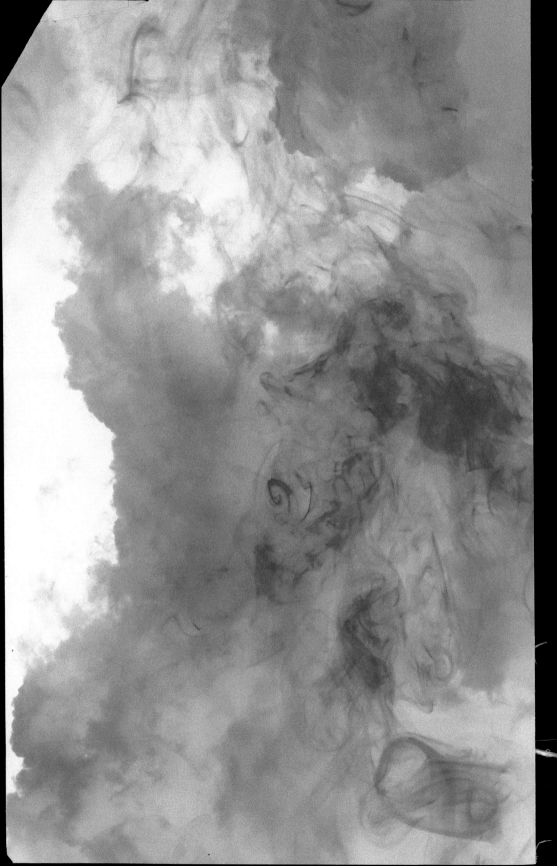

# CANDLE MAGIC

## FOR BEGINNERS

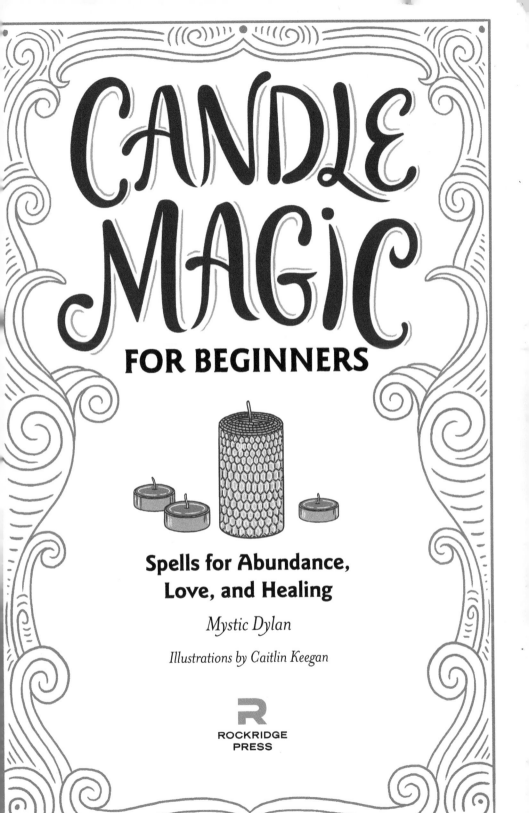

### Spells for Abundance, Love, and Healing

*Mystic Dylan*

*Illustrations by Caitlin Keegan*

**ROCKRIDGE PRESS**

Interior and Cover Designers: Michael Patti and Angela Navarra
Art Producer: Hannah Dickerson
Editor: Sean Newcott
Production Manager: Giraud Lorber
Production Editor: Melissa Edeburn

Illustrations © 2020 Caitlin Keegan. All other images used under license from Shutterstock.com. Author photo courtesy of Olivia Graves.

ISBN: Print 978-1-64739-841-5 | eBook 978-1-64739-537-7
R1

To the ancestors who paved this
path for us, those who choose to follow,
and those who have yet to discover it.

# "CURIOSITY IS THE WICK IN THE CANDLE OF LEARNING."

—*William Arthur Ward*

# Candle Magic & You

If you're reading this book, you've likely felt the pull of candle magic. Perhaps you've sensed the power held inside the wax, wick, and flame, and you want to explore it further. If you are looking to start a magical practice or try spellwork, you couldn't find a better tool to begin with than the candle. Candles allow us to focus our intentions and tap into our creativity. No matter how big or small your goal, candle magic is a wonderful way to access transformational energy.

*Candle Magic for Beginners* doesn't just cover how to use candles for magic; it explains how to develop a relationship with magic through the candle. Within these pages, you'll learn the history and significance of fire, what exactly candle magic entails, and how to safely and sustainably develop a practice. You'll learn how to set and manifest intentions; how to choose, cleanse, charge, and **consecrate** candles for magic; how to tell if your spell is working; and how to **scry**, or read, the flame and wax. You'll put this new knowledge into action with 30 spells that speak to love, protection, healing, prosperity, and well-being.

If you're at the start of your magical journey, know that I was once in the same place. Growing up, I split my time between living with my (divorced) parents on the West Coast and my grandparents on the East Coast. Despite the occasional chaos and drama, my family always instilled in me the wonder, fantasy, and knowledge that magic requires. My father read me stories of epic adventures, divine gods, and enchanting beasts from mythology. My grandmother taught me the power of prayer, told me stories of angels, and introduced me to yoga and meditation. My grandfather educated me about history and influenced my love of ancient Egypt.

And my mother took me on my first trip to a metaphysical shop, which solidified my spiritual practice and craft. She and I celebrated my ninth birthday with a trip to Panpipes (now called Pan's Apothika) in Hollywood, where I met Vicky, an ethereal red-haired woman in a black dress. She was seated behind the counter, carving a candle, surrounded by the most incredible array of herbs, incense, and oils.

Suddenly, she looked up at me and smiled. I grabbed my mother's hand and knew I was in the presence of a real witch. My mother may not have known it then, but that day marked the start of my own journey as a budding witch. I was entranced: I'd always known that magic was real, but I now knew that magic was practiced!

I got my first candles, oils, and herbs at Panpipes—but candles were my first introduction to hands-on magic. When I was younger, candles allowed me to do spellwork and rituals at home without drawing anyone's attention. As I honed my craft, I began to do more spells, make mini-altars, and incorporate candles into my daily routine. It became clear to me during those formative years that the candle was much more than a religious token or symbol of devotion; it was a beacon of power, a way to navigate desires, wishes, and manifestations.

Candles have always been the primary tool in my craft. From carving the candle to anointing and lighting it, I immerse myself in the ritual, thus creating an energetic bond and bringing life to the candle and spell.

When I started working as a professional witch in enchantment shops, I often found that clients were surprised to learn that many of their desires could be fulfilled and spell requests achieved through the use of a single candle. I was always excited to teach them, and I'm excited to teach you, too.

Let us begin.

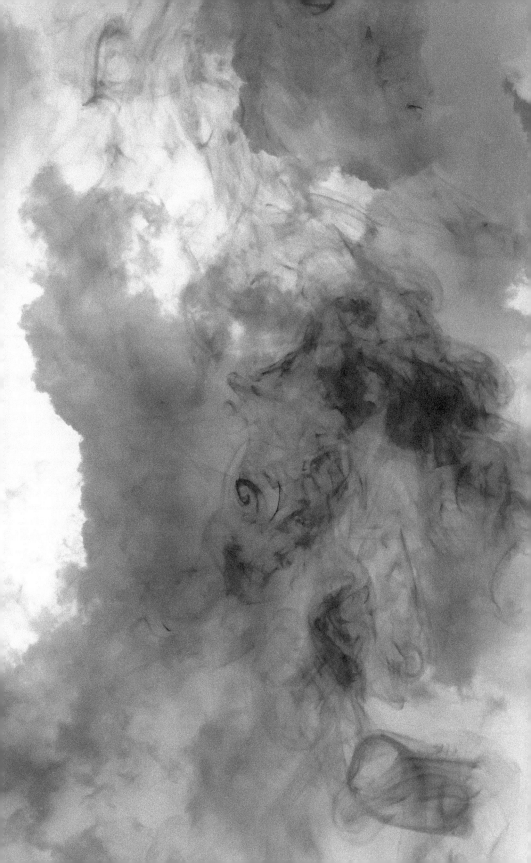

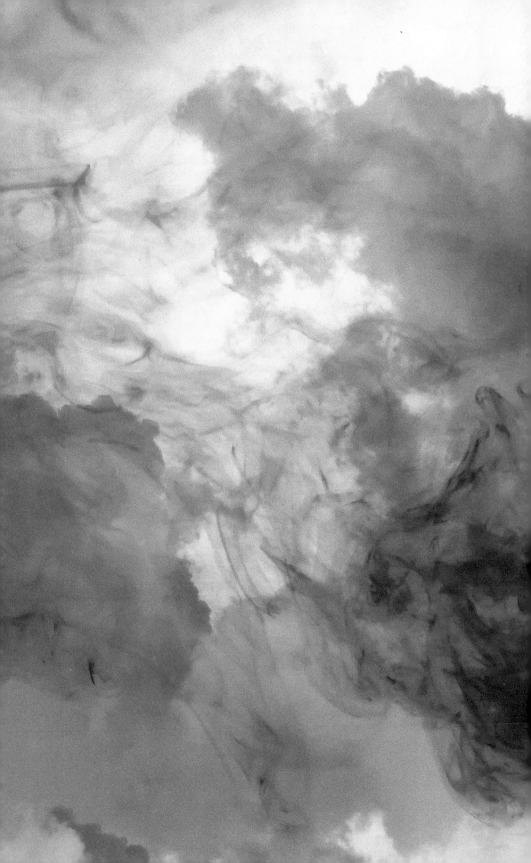

*Part One*

# THE POWER
# OF FIRE &
# TRANSFORMATION

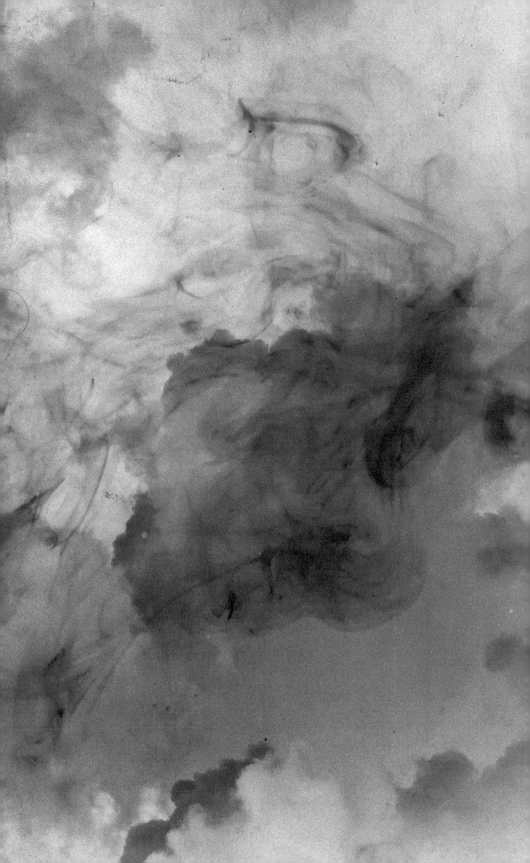

## CHAPTER ONE

# ILLUMINATING CANDLE MAGIC

Before we light our first candles,
we have to understand how candle magic works as well
as how candles became such powerful
and evergreen tools in the craft. We must first go
back centuries to discover humanity's rich
relationship with fire.

# The Ancient Power of Fire

The history of fire is steeped in **magic**. When humans first ground stones together some 400,000 years ago, making the spark that lit the first fire, they paved the way for a complete change in human existence. Mastery of the flames allowed our ancestors to live in cold climates, revolutionize cooking, and illuminate the darkness. Fire gave them a place to huddle together and share stories, dance, and connect to the earth and supernatural realm.

Our ancestors considered fire critically important, which is why there are so many myths linked to it—most famously, the ancient Greek story of Prometheus, who stole fire from the gods and gave it to man. This myth spoke to fire as something primordial, divine, and truly magical. When it wasn't tamed by humans, fire was an unruly element that caused pain, devastation, and death. Fire was revered for its duality.

When fire was controlled, it became a symbol of power, and it was used as such in many magical and spiritual customs. The ancient Greeks and Romans performed sacred cremations, placing the deceased on **pyres** and setting them on fire.

Pyres were also used for sacred fires at **altars**, where animals were burned as offerings to the **deity**. Ceremonial bonfires played a similarly important role in **rituals** across many cultures, such as the Celtic holidays of Samhain and Beltane. During these holidays, which respectively mark the dark and light halves of the year, Celts and Druids lit bonfires on hilltops and used them as a form of sympathetic magic—the bonfires were meant to represent the sun and dispel the decay and darkness of winter. The flames were intended to destroy harmful influences; in some rituals, people even leapt through the flames in order to be purified by the fire. In southern Louisiana, the custom of ritual bonfires remains. On Christmas Eve, bonfires are built along the Mississippi River to light the way for Papa Noël, who is pulled on the river in his pirogue (Cajun canoe) by eight alligators.

Eventually, fire was contained in the hearth of homes and used as a source of warmth and protection. For those practicing magic at that time, fire was used to heat ingredients in a cauldron, a common witchcraft tool. But candles were not yet commonplace. In fact, the candle as we think of it today didn't exist until the Middle Ages. There are records of the ancient Egyptians making candles out of rushlights (a candle made from the pith of a rush plant soaked in some kind of fat) and beeswax as early as 3000 BCE, but beeswax was very expensive due to the dangers associated with cultivating it. The Native Americans of the Pacific Northwest used the candlefish, an oily, edible fish that could be dried and used as candles or torches. In Japan, people used wax from whale fat as an alternative to beeswax, but prior to the Middle Ages, most magic practitioners used oil lamps instead of candles. Lamps were used for **divination**, rituals, and spellwork in Greece, Rome, and Egypt, and in ancient Judeo-Christian customs. Today, oil lamps still play a role in the rituals of some cultures. Oil lamps are used in Afro-Caribbean practices, and in the oldest types of workings in New Orleans Voodoo and Hoodoo.

Tallow, which is made from animal fat, was used to craft candles in the Middle Ages. The use of tallow made candles more accessible, and they soon became a household item.

During the Middle Ages, candles also became more commonly used in magic—though not necessarily by witches. One of the first-recorded instances of candles being used for magical purposes occurred during the witch hunts. During the Middle Ages and Renaissance, more than 80,000 people who were suspected of practicing witchcraft in Europe were put to death by the church. A 1486 handbook for inquisitors and witch hunters called the *Malleus Maleficarum* claimed that a holy candle was one of the consecrated objects that could be used for "preserving oneself from the injury of witches." Candles were also used by farmers and country folk to protect their livestock and homes from bewitchment. In older Jewish customs, candles were lit for the dying and placed at their bedsides to ward off demons. The custom of lighting candles for loved ones and hoping to catch the attention and divine wisdom of God was later adopted within Christianity and incorporated into Catholicism.

In many ways, the history of modern candle magic begins with Catholicism. Documents from Catholic Spiritualists show the candle itself was considered divine and the burning of the candle viewed as a sacrifice. These philosophies and practices are still implemented in candle magic.

By the late 19th century, an inexpensive wax called paraffin began to be used to create high-quality candles. Paraffin wax replaced tallow because paraffin candles were easier to produce and smelled much better. The introduction of paraffin allowed candles to be manufactured for commercial use. By the late 1930s and early 1940s, candles were regarded as a standard magical tool, often required for use in ritual, prayer, séances, or spellwork. Psychics, shamans, healers, witch doctors, and Vodou mambos were harnessing the power of the candle and prescribing its use to clients and patients. Candles were an especially useful magical tool because they were common and discreet enough to prevent practitioners from being outed as witches, or heathens, to the church.

Starting in the 16th century, the Atlantic slave trade led to the intermingling of Catholicism and African traditions in the Caribbean, Cuba, and New Orleans, birthing a new spiritual faith. African, Native American, and European folk practices merged with Catholicism to create several different religions and spiritual customs. Various styles of candle magic eventually made their way across America and were incorporated into many other beliefs and magical practices.

Today, candle magic is used in spells and rituals all over the world. Candle magic does not belong to any one specific tradition or religion; rather, it has transcended and taken root as a core part of magic.

# The Foundation of Candle Magic

Why have candles become a primary tool in the modern-day witch's repertoire? Aside from how accessible and inexpensive candles often are, they are also available in a wide variety of shapes, sizes, colors, materials, and scents. You can even make your own. Candles are versatile; they can be used in a variety of spiritual and magical practices, from lighting your sacred space to serving as the star of your ritual and spellwork. You can **anoint** candles with oils and enchant them to gain protection. Candles are also carved and charged to secure financial stability, or pricked with pins to influence a potential lover or client. After the candle has finished burning, its magic is still prevalent. You can use the remnants of candle wax as a powerful **talisman**, or gaze into the shapes made by melted wax to decipher the outcome of your spellwork. Although the candle itself is imbued with strong magic, its essence and enchantment can be greatly magnified with the use of essential oils and sacred herbs.

A candle is a torch to the divine, a conduit to the other realm, and a beacon of magic and enchantment. Not only does the candle harness potent magic, but the process of burning is ritualistic in itself. When you use a candle in spellwork or a ritual, you are utilizing the power of the four elements. Like the great alchemists of old, you are wielding a transformative energy. Simply lighting the candle enacts its base element—fire—connecting us to the primordial gift given to us by the great Titan Prometheus. It is the sacred communion with air that feeds this flame and allows the enticing dance to begin, ultimately achieving our desires. The candle wax represents stability and strength, because melted candle wax resembles a tree trunk. Like a tree's roots, the candle wax connects you to the earth and keeps your intentions grounded. As the flame dances and the wax begins to melt, the candle, a pillar of strength, changes from its solid form to become one with the element of water, connecting to our emotional desires and merging all elements into one. Once the candle has melted and transformed, the fifth and final element—spirit—appears. If you use your intuition, you can even peer into the images the wax has left behind and understand the hidden language of the candle.

# Fire for Illumination, Elimination & Transformation

Lighting the wick of a candle is not a mundane act; you are unleashing the primordial essence of the flame itself. The candle becomes more than just the physical representation of your desire; it also houses and attracts the spirit, or the energy, that will assist you in achieving your goal. I encourage you to stare at the flame of a candle to unlock your subconscious and release your spiritual self. The candle has the power to purge your fears, eliminate negativity, and transform you into the divine being you're meant to be. As you pursue candle magic, never forget that the candle unleashes powerful energy that is fueled and magnified by its relationship with you.

# Magic Flows Where Intention Goes

As you've learned, candles represent the four elements—air, earth, water, fire—which make candles the go-to tool for harnessing and connecting with the energies of the universe. But remember that simply lighting the candle is not enough. The key to candle magic is intention. You must first focus on your intention and infuse that into the candle, charging it with the energy and passion that lives in your soul. Charging a candle with intention is what gives the candle and spell life. When you give a piece of your soul to the working, this intention **conjures** up spirit.

# You Know That's Magic, Right?

As you delve deeper in your practice, you'll begin to notice that candle magic exists all around you. Think about when you make a wish and blow out the candles on a birthday cake—that's magic. When you light a candle for a loved one in need, that's magic, too. Even the candles placed in jack-o'-lanterns on Halloween have roots that connect back to magic and folklore.

# Lighting the Way

The spark of creation has been ignited—now it's time to fan that spark into a true flame. Candle magic is a powerful practice, and a wonderful way to begin your magical and spiritual journey. Next, you'll learn about the significance of candle colors as well as their corresponding qualities and spells.

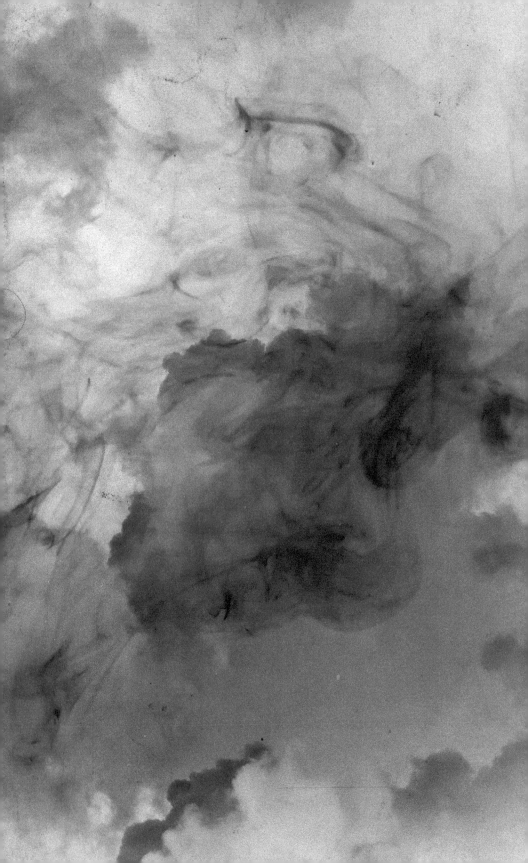

## CHAPTER TWO

# CANDLE COLOR CORRESPONDENCES

In this chapter, you will delve into the importance of colors and the magic that can be harnessed from them. These color correspondences derive from a blend of Hoodoo, folk magic, and traditional witchcraft, and will assist you in choosing the right candle for your magical workings. Many different colors exist in the natural world and each color has a specific meaning. Here you'll be acquainted with the common colors used in candle magic and their unique meanings.

# The Power of Color

Choosing the appropriate candle color is vital when performing candle magic, or rituals of any kind. Every color has an essence, promotes a feeling, and gives off a specific energy. By choosing a specific color, you are setting the tone for your spell and desired outcome. With color alone, you can control the narrative of what you hope to accomplish in your spellwork. An appropriately chosen colored candle can not only lock in your spellwork with intentions and meanings, but also enhance elemental properties, bring about desired qualities, and attract specific spirits and deities.

In the following pages, you'll explore the many mysteries and messages that lay within the standard candle colors. Keep in mind that although these color correspondences are a wonderful reference, especially for a novice or beginner, choosing a color should ultimately align with your personal feelings and associations with that color. For example, I'm not a fan of the colors orange and yellow. So, even though they have powerful and positive associations, I will look for those associations and strengths in other colors that resonate with me, such as purple and blue.

## Red

Red is the color of blood, our life-force, vitality, attraction, sensuality, desire, ambition, virility, and strength. Red is the color of birth and death, of fire and earth, violence and love, sex and healing. It is considered by many to be the most magical color due to its balanced properties and connection to primordial and ancestral energies. Red is the sacred color of the goddesses Isis and Lilith and is associated with deep magic (primordial or chaos magic that does not take into account ideas of good or bad, and dark or light). The color red also corresponds to Aries and is linked with Mars. Red candles can be used in spells regarding vitality, strength, and health. They can also be used in spellwork focused on achieving goals, overcoming obstacles, or **sex magic** (any type of sexual activity used for magical, ritualistic, or spiritual purposes). This prominent color is also useful for gaining luck or courage in situations when you need a little more attention on your-self. Though a popular choice for love spells, keep in mind that the color red exudes a very sexual energy; if you are seeking long-term romance, monogamy, or marriage, make sure that the intention is clear. You may want to dress, or anoint, a red candle with herbs such as rose or jasmine to subdue those fiery qualities and balance it with tranquility, love, harmony, and romance. You might also prefer to substitute a subtler pink candle instead—pink is best suited for romance and monogamy. In ancient Greece, red was considered a color of life and was used in rituals of necromancy to speak to spirits. Red was also used to combat outside forces like malevolent spirits or enemies. Red apples, pome-granates, toadstools, and berries were all considered foods of the Greek and Roman gods, so you can implement a red candle in spellwork to entice deities and spirits to assist in your workings.

## Orange

Orange promotes positive energy, exuberance, and courage, and is linked to the power of the sun. It is associated with the planet Mercury and the element of fire. This color is useful in spellwork for obtaining positive outcomes, job successes, and wish fulfillment. If you are being considered for a new job or wish to be professionally noticed within a larger group, use orange candles in spells to stand out from the rest. Because orange represents the turning of the leaves in fall, it can also be utilized in spells dealing with change, transforma-tion, and alchemy.

## Yellow

Yellow exudes brilliance, joy, and clarity. It is also linked to solar deities such as Apollo, Horus, and Mithras. Use yellow candles to promote clairvoyance, insight, or when you're seeking the truth in spellwork. Yellow is also a popular candle color for unhexing, uncrossing, and protection spells. You can employ yellow candles when seeking healing guidance, or to brighten your mood and expel depres-sion. Overall, yellow can be used for rituals that invoke happiness and encourage healing from an operation or illness.

## Green

Nowadays, green is most commonly associated with money, abundance, and greed; to the ancient Egyptians, however, it was the color of life, fertility, and youth. Green is the sacred color of Osiris, Cernunnos, Pan, Ogun, and Demeter. In Celtic folklore, green is also associated with fairies and their magic, which connects us to the otherworld (a supernatural realm that's somewhat parallel to our own, where deities, spirits, fae, and our dead commingle). Earth and Venus are the fixed planets for the color green, and water and earth are the color's associated elements. Green is also associated with Taurus. This color exudes strong vibrations of luck, prosperity, and wealth. Green energy is also potent for those wishing to bear children, and in turn can be used for fertility and sex magic. Green represents the bounty of the earth and the riches supplied to us by Mother Nature. It is the perfect color for spellwork and rituals that seek financial growth, stability, luck, abundance, and success. Green can also be used in spellwork to counter jealousy, ambition, greed, and theft.

## Indigo

Indigo is a deep, rich color found on the same part of the spectrum as the color blue. Indigo corresponds to the planets Saturn and Venus and is sacred to the goddess Isis and the Virgin Mary. It is associated with renewal, relaxation, reflection, and the easing of tension. This color can be used in spellwork and rituals that require meditation and trance work or used to welcome new beginnings and conduct house blessings.

## Blue

Blue is an ethereal color that connects to the heavenly and divine. Blue is sacred to Zeus, Yemaya, Mary, and Nut, the Egyptian goddess of the sky and heavens. Blue's associated element is water. Blue candles can be used in magical workings to promote strength in healing spells. Blue also neutralizes intense vibrations and can be used to induce a sense of peace and tranquility, which makes it a popular candle color for house cleansings and energy work. Blue **novena** or pullout candles can be used to petition saints and deities for specific workings.

## Pink

The color pink is the essence of true love. Sacred to Aphrodite, Venus, and Erzulie, it is the color of emotional love, representing affection, compassion, beauty, and fidelity. Pink candles can be used in spellwork to promote romantic relationships, monogamy, and marriage as well as in rituals to attract new love and happiness. The color pink can also be useful to temper and heal feuds between friends, dispel anger, and promote a sense of harmony in relationships.

## Purple

Purple, the color of royalty and the divine, is also the color of power and the supernatural. When you come across purple flowers, that is a blessing from the deities above. Purple is sacred to Maman Brigitte, Dionysus, Bacchus, and the Ghede, which are Voudon loas, or spirits of sex, fertility, and death. Purple candles can be used in spellwork that requires a lot of energy. They're also useful in spells to gain personal or financial independence, or when you feel that your desired goal may be difficult to achieve. Purple is also a high vibrational color and, therefore, well-suited for spirit work, trance meditation, and astral travel. Burn purple candles for psychic insight and when performing divination.

## Brown

Brown represents the earth, both the element and the planet itself. Because of its strong vibrations of strength and balance, you can use brown candles to draw upon stability. This color works well in spellwork for justice, earth magic, animal and pet spells, and attracting nature spirits. You can also use the color brown in rituals for grounding and level-headedness, or whenever you need strength and courage to make a difficult decision or choice.

## Gray

Gray represents the liminal place between worlds, or the veil that divides humans from the unknown. Gray is sacred to the Fates and the Graeae (Gray Sisters) as well as to Mercury and Athena. Gray is connected to the element of air and can also be used for ancestral work or travel. Gray candles are best used in spells for spirit communication and necromancy, and to neutralize negative energy. You can also implement gray in spells for communication, knowledge, and wisdom. Light a gray candle when studying or reading to assist in retaining knowledge, or burn a gray candle in a home to gain an awareness of the spirits that might reside within.

## Black

The color black's association with evil and baneful magic is based in bias and cultural racism. Though some perceive magic using the color black as evil, dirty, and primitive, and magic incorporating the color white as good, pure, and clean, this belief is incorrect. In reality, black has actually represented life in many cultures throughout history. It is the color of the dark and waning moon; sacred to Hecate, Nyx, and Diana; and associated with the planet Saturn and the elements earth and water. A color of wisdom and death, black symbolizes resurrection and renewal. Because it is the absence of light and contains all colors, black is a wonderful color to use for absorbing and deflecting negative energy, spirits, curses, and **hexes**. Black candles can be used in spells for binding, banishing, uncrossing, and exorcism.

## White

The absence of color makes white one of the strongest colors for spellwork and beyond. This color is connected to the spiritual realm, innocence, wonder, purity, and new beginnings. White is sacred to Hathor, Cerridwen, Isis, Chango, and the Triple Goddess, and connected to the moon and all five elements—earth, water, fire, air, and spirit. Since it is the same color as milk, white is often linked to life, fertility, and nourishment; in many folk magic practices, white is known as a highly symbolic color of goodness and balance. White is also the color of bone, linking it with death and structure. The color of snow, white can be used to freeze other energies or disturbances and as protection from outside forces. In general, you can think of the color white as a blank canvas ready to be transformed; it is the beginning and the end. White candles can be utilized in spells for clarity, protection, meditation, and angel magic. Light a white candle to attract inspiration and creativity, or to create a sacred space.

## Gold

The color gold contains male god energy, specifically that which is linked with the sun. The gods Apollo, Ra, Horus, Mithras, and Oshun are all connected to gold. The solar energy of gold corresponds to fire and is utilized in spellwork for abundance, prosperity, attraction, and money. Incorporate the color gold into rituals to call on the divine masculine, or to influence someone or something. If you are in negotiations for a project, implement a gold candle into your working to attract an employer or client and get their attention.

## Silver

Silver, the color of the divine feminine, is sacred to all lunar goddesses and thus is imbued with lunar properties; it can be used to represent any moon phase required in a spell. Use silver candles for spells regarding psychic work, money, financial stability, peace, protection, and spiritual guidance, as well as spells to enhance spellwork and spiritual wisdom. Silver can also be used in rituals to promote clairvoyance, motherhood, and marriage.

# Color Variations

As you build your candle tool kit, you'll discover that there's a wide variety of shades to choose from for each color. Though different shades may have different vibrations, picking the "wrong" shade is not something to be afraid of. If a spell calls for deep purple, it won't ruin your spellwork to use a different shade such as lavender. Keep in mind, however, that shades do create variations; lavender still contains purple's traits of prophecy and insight, but its vibrations are more soothing than deep purple's and are commonly used for meditation and sleep. It is best to choose the appropriate color that connects with you and then see what options are available within the different shades. A good rule of thumb is that the darker the color, the more intense the energy; conversely, a subtler shade will yield a subtler result. Here are a few color variations you may encounter and how to best use them.

**Bright Blue:** Used to avert the evil eye, electric blue can be implemented for justice and attracting air elementals (spirits).

**Dark Blue:** Dark blue is sacred to Hades and Neptune and connected to the planets Jupiter and Saturn. This color connects with the element of water and can be used for sea magic. It can also be used in spells that require emotional strength and mental clarity.

**Magenta:** This color is useful for spellwork concerning mental healing, recovery, and spiritual awakening.

**Wine/Maroon:** A popular color in Voodoo and Santería, this deep shade is sacred to the Orishas and Loas, and represents the blessings of the earth, magical workings, and sex magic.

**Emerald Green:** The deep green color can be implemented in any type of spellwork to promote growth, abundance, and financial success. Emerald green corresponds to Venus and can also be used to find stable, monogamous love.

**Dark Green/Hunter Green:** An even deeper, darker shade of green, dark or hunter green can be used in spells to ward off jealousy and end financial disputes. These shades can also be used to assist in spells or rituals to win court cases or lawsuits.

**WITCH TIP**

## *Candles for Broad Spellwork*

There's a wide variety of colored candles out there to choose from, so don't feel obligated to collect them all. If you find that a spell calls for a specific color that you're missing and there's no corresponding color in your kit that fits your working, simply substitute a black or white candle. Black is a combination of all colors and therefore can be utilized in any working to take on the desired vibration. Black also banishes and wards off negativity, making it a great all-purpose candle. White is the absence of color and corresponds to all four elements, so it can be used as a substitute for any color required for a specific spell or ritual. (It's also one of the easiest colored candles to find.) The color white's link to the divine and celestial realm also makes it the ideal candidate for a traditional all-purpose candle. Whether you're using a black or white candle, think of your intent and go with the vibration that bests suits you and your desired outcome.

# Lighting the Way

Think of colors as the visual component of energy. When focusing on the desired outcome you wish to gain from spellwork, imagine what that goal looks like, color-wise. As you explore the different colors and become acquainted with their vibrations and meanings, you'll be able to find the color that best suits your spell. When deciding on a color, you can also think of any deities, planetary signs, or elements you wish to work with—utilizing their specific colors will enhance the properties of the spell. But color isn't the only thing to be aware of. In the next chapter, you will be introduced to the wide variety of candle shapes and sizes and learn the benefits of each one for your magical practice.

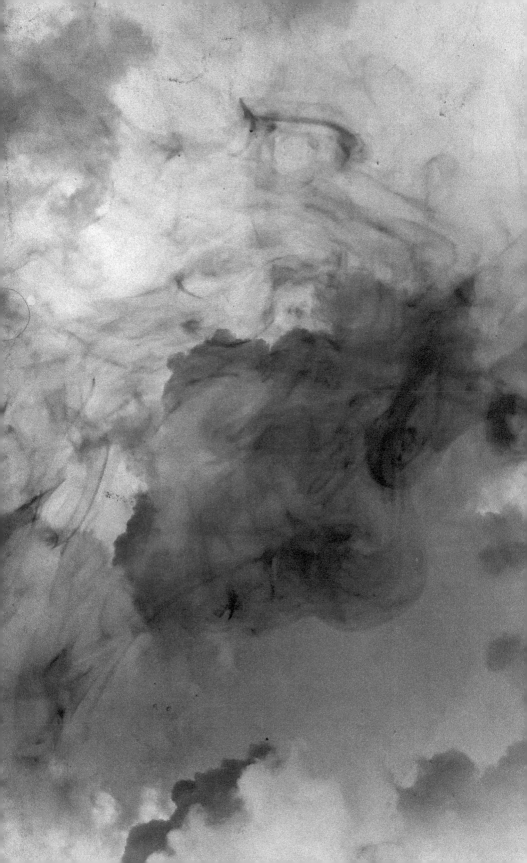

## CHAPTER THREE

# CURATING CANDLES FOR MAGIC

In this chapter, you will explore various candle shapes, sizes, and burn times, and how those factors contribute to candle magic. You will also learn what candles to use for specific rituals or spells, and how to best prepare for the spellwork and magical workings to come.

# To Each Their Own Candle

If you are just beginning your candle magic journey, I find that it is best to have a variety of candle options at your disposal. Acquiring different shapes, sizes, and colors of candles, as well as a collection of herbs and oils, will give you the freedom to whip up a spell at any moment. Now, I'm not encouraging you to go on a shopping spree (although that can be fun), but I do suggest thinking about any spellwork or rituals you may want to perform in the future and prepping any necessary materials. It's also good to have a few basic candles on hand, such as votives or pillars, so you can easily craft when the opportunity presents itself. There's nothing more stressful than searching last minute for the candles and tools you need so you can complete a spell on time during a full moon.

There are many different ways you can curate your candle magic tool kit: You can collect a variety of colors after referencing the color correspondence in the previous chapter, or you can keep stock of a particular candle and color as you focus on one specific working at a time. You will discover over the course of reading this book that not all rituals and spells call for a specific type of candle; in that case, you should choose whichever one suits the magical working best. These are the moments when you must tap into your intuition and feel what candle gives off the strongest vibration in relation to your chosen spell or ritual—which is precisely why having a variety of candles in your tool kit will come in handy!

## Votive Candles

**Burn time:** 10 to 15 hours

A typical votive candle is about two inches in height and fits into a glass or ceramic votive holder. You can use a votive candle without a holder for a shorter burn time, or if you want to do wax divination after your spell. These candles come in a variety of colors, are often sold in packs, and can be purchased for a reasonable price, making them a suitable option for a beginner's candle magic tool kit.

## Novena/Vigil Candles

**Burn time:** 7 to 9 days

Also called the 7-day candle, novena or **vigil** candles are probably the most well-known and accessible candle out there. They are especially popular in Hoodoo, Voodoo, folk magic, and Santería. Novena candles come in several versions and styles: some have labels associated with Catholic saints, some may have good luck symbols or words printed on the glass, and others are plain and don't feature any images at all. Novena candles come in a variety of colors and work well for dressing—you can draw **sigils** and words of power onto their glass container with a permanent marker for additional energy, and they are so tall that you can easily fill them with oils and herbs. These candles are intended to burn all the way down without interruptions, but you can place them in a sink, bathtub, or shower if you wish to contain the flame and take extra precautions.

## Tealight Candles

**Burn time:** 3 hours

Tealights are a worthwhile yet affordable investment; these candles are widely available, sold in a variety of colors, and sold in large packs. Tealights are perfect for making ritual circles or creating altars to enhance spellwork. To conjure up some quick and easy magic, you can drop a bit of scented oil and a sprinkle of herbs onto the tops of the tealights. A few of these candles in your tool kit will enable you to experience magic on the go.

## Beeswax Candles

**Burn time:** 60 + hours

Beeswax has a long history in magic. Beeswax was once rare and also dangerous to acquire, which only added to its candle's mystery and spiritual potency. Beeswax is a natural material and burns longer, making it a luxury item among modern candle magic practitioners; however, due to its cost, it may not be ideal for simple spellwork. Beeswax candles come in many forms, sizes, and colors and can be rolled, poured, or dipped. These candles are best used for longer rituals that require stronger vibrations and intent.

## Soy Candles

**Burn time:** 5 to 10 hours

Soy candles are natural and sometimes preferred by those working with earth magic. They retain scents very well but tend to have shorter burn times than beeswax candles. They can also be very brittle and difficult to mold or carve when dressing. Most soy candles are found already encased in glass. They are best used for spells regarding healing and renewal, or to call on nature spirits and faes.

## Seven-Knob Candles

**Burn time:** 7 days

Seven-knob candles, which are molded with seven round knobs stacked on top of one another, have been popular among practitioners of African folk magic, con- jure, and Voodoo since the 1930s. The standard practice with a seven-knob candle is to dedicate each knob to a wish— you can choose a different wish for each knob or use the same wish for all of them. You then carve each knob with your wish, along with the sigils or initials of the person you are doing the working for. Then, dress the candles with oil and/or herbs and burn for seven nights, one knob per night, pinching or **snuffing** the flame out (never blowing it out) when the spell is complete. This candle is a wonderful edition to your tool kit, especially for multi-day workings.

## Pullout Candles

**Burn time:** 3 to 7 days

Similar to the novena/vigil candles, pullout candles are typically eight-and-a-half inches tall and come inside a glass holder that's the same size and shape of the candle. But unlike novenas, pullout candles can also be removed from the glass and used on their own—hence their name. These candles are perfect for a variety of spells and rituals. They can be carved and dressed with oils; herbs can be put directly into the bottom of the glass, with the candle placed on top and left to burn out completely. These candles, which have become popular due to their efficiency and how easy it is to personalize them, are essential for any candle magic tool kit.

## Chime Candles

**Burn time:** 90 minutes to 2 hours

Chime candles are a must-have for any practitioner, especially a novice or beginner. They are four inches tall and come in a variety of colors, can be easily carved for spellwork, and burn down quickly, so they work well for multiple workings and spells. You can typically purchase them at a very reasonable price—a single chime candle will usually cost one to two dollars. These are easily the best candles to have on hand in your tool kit.

## Figure Candles

**Burn time:** Depends on the figure

Another tool popular among modern candle magic practitioners, figure candles are shaped like people, animals, or other shapes, and used in sympathetic magic, a form of spellwork based on the principle that "like attracts like." So, the specific shape of the candle attracts the desired outcome. For example, a black cat candle would be utilized to attract luck and ward off **jinxes**, whereas a male or female figure candle could be used to represent a specific person you wish to attract, heal, or influence.

## Pillar Candles

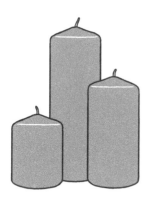

**Burn time:** 30 to 35 hours

Pillar candles are widely available, but they have been replaced by pullout candles in modern candle magic. If pillar candles are your last resort or preference, feel free to use them. They are great for setting intentions for long-term goals and work well in spells or rituals guided by lunar phases or planetary hours, or those that last multiple days or weeks. Pillar candles are great for carving and are available in a variety of colors and sizes.

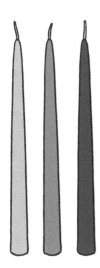

## Taper Candles

**Burn time:** 12 hours

Taper candles are distinguished by their long, narrow shape and conical top. They are best used when performing rituals, for simple intention settings, or for attraction spells. They are fragile and have messy burn cycles that result in a lot of dripping wax, so they are not the best candidates for carving or hands-on spellwork—but they work well for candle divination. Dress taper candles with jasmine, lavender, or other love attraction oils and burn them during a date to promote love and attraction. Because taper candles are so tall, they are typically burned in sections over the course of several days. Use colors such as gold or silver for celestial and divine assistance as well as money workings.

## Homemade Candles

Though making your own candles is by no means necessary, homemade candles are a great way to create a spell from the ground up and set higher and stronger vibrations. If you want to make your own candles, an online tutorial can help you pick out the necessary tools and equipment, learn different candle-making methods, and assist you on your crafting journey. If you are interested in homemade candles but don't have the ability to make them yourself, you can look into a shop that offers homemade candles and other ritual tools crafted by fellow witches.

# Fragrance

Much like colors, scents have their own vibrations and magical benefits, too. A challenge you may encounter with scented color candles is that the magical correspondence may not match up. So, always use your intuition when choosing scents. If you are performing a multi-day ritual, or a spell that requires the candle to burn down instead of being extinguished, make sure that the scent will not disturb you or others in your household or workspace. Many practitioners choose to dress or anoint their own candles with fragrance. However, I find that fragrance not only adds a more personal touch to the working, but also enhances the vibrations and effectiveness of the spellwork. Just a drop or two of essential oil rubbed into the candle or dressed on top can work wonders.

# Burn Time

In this book, and throughout your practice, you will find that certain spells and rituals require different lengths of time and dedication. Therefore, make sure you factor in burn time when choosing a candle for a spell. A tealight or votive is probably not the best foundation for a multi-day spell, unless you want to continuously replenish the candle. If a spell requires the candle to burn down completely without being extinguished, think practically about the time and attention you are able to give to the spell. If you're unable to oversee the complete burning down of a candle, be mindful not to leave it burning unattended; choose a chime candle instead of a larger candle, due to its short burn time. If you're doing a bigger working, consider a pullout or novena candle that is protected by glass and thus safer than a taper or other unprotected candle.

# Discovering Candles

In general, candles are easily accessible, which is part of what makes them so popular in witchcraft, Voodoo, Hoodoo, Wicca, and other spiritual workings. Many of the candles mentioned in this chapter can be found online as well as in drug stores, grocery stores, and even the dollar store. Candles made primarily for magic or spiritual purposes such as figure candles, pullouts, and seven-knob candles can be found in metaphysical shops, botanicas, witchcraft shops, or online.

Keep in mind that your candle's power or usage is the same no matter where you bought it. Whether the novena candle was purchased at the dollar store or the metaphysical shop does not have any bearing on the power of the candle—only the price. Though you may want to support your local metaphysical shop, ultimately, the magic comes from within you.

# Lighting the Way

You're now familiar with the wonderful array of candles that you can collect and use, and the magic that can be accomplished with them. But before you delve into spell casting, you must first ready the candle—it's time for some hands-on sorcery. In the next chapter, you will learn how to properly prepare a candle for spellwork and rituals.

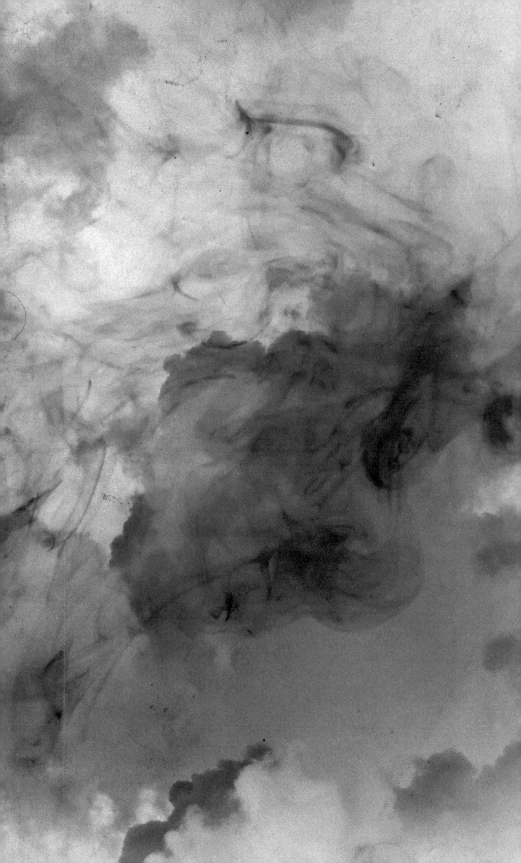

## CHAPTER FOUR

# CLEANSING, CHARGING & CONSECRATING CANDLES

In this chapter, you'll learn how to create a sacred space and cleanse a candle as well as the importance of candle consecration and how to understand appropriate burning time. These are all necessary spiritual steps that not only enhance the magical properties of the candles for spellwork, but also awaken the energetic vibrations deep within.

# Creating a Space Worthy of Candle Magic

When performing candle magic or any other type of spellwork, many practitioners prefer to have a sacred space dedicated to magic or ritual. This space is known as an altar—a special space designated for magic where you can set up your candles and perform your spells. An altar can be set up on a table, bookshelf, trunk, or even the top of a dresser. Some witches and practitioners will redecorate their altar to suit different seasons or holidays, or to honor specific deities and spirits. Feel free to decorate your altar with crystals, feathers, flowers, pictures, statues, and colored candles that correspond to whatever you wish to celebrate or honor. As you'll find in this book and others like it, many spells suggest working with a deity or spirit, so it might boost your spellwork to incorporate elements of that deity or spirit into your altar.

When setting up an altar, safety always comes first. Make sure your altar space is clear of electrical cords, phone chargers, or any other obstructive clutter. When burning candles on your altar, make sure they are kept away from fabric, paper, or any other flammable materials. If you are burning chime candles, tapers, or votives, make sure they are in holders or on a heatproof dish. Always have a bowl, cup, or glass of water on hand. Water will not only extinguish any flames that get out of hand but can invite spirits to assist in your workings.

One way to always keep your altar clean is to prep your candles in a separate area such as the kitchen. In my own workspace, I have a designated portable serving tray as my candle station; I carve, dress, and prep candles there before putting them on my altar, so that the tray can catch the wax, oil, glitter, and any other mess I might make. Another simple solution is to use a cardboard box as a candle station.

# Cleansing Candles

Cleansing is an important part of any magical process; it's the means by which you clear your candle, tools, and space of negative, stagnant, and preexisting energies. You always want your tools to feel fresh so that their vibrations are at their highest and most potent. Cleansing is a ritual in itself, and is found throughout most spiritual and magical practices. There are many different methods of cleansing, but I have found that smoke cleansing or smudging—or as I like to call it, "spiritual fumigation"—is the most effective method. Exposure to the magical/cleansing properties of the herbs, resins, woods, or incense that's being burned will also enhance your candle.

**To conduct a cleansing ritual, follow these easy steps:**

1. Decide what you'd like to cleanse your candle with. You can use herbs, woods, or incense such as frankincense, myrrh, palo santo, sage, sweetgrass, rosemary, or cedar. Your personal preference takes precedence here. If you can't decide, consider what spiritual path you follow, and what spirits/deities you are working with.

2. Light the chosen incense and wait for it to smoke. (If you are using frankincense or myrrh, you will need to burn these on a charcoal disk and incense burner.) As the incense begins to smoke and smolder, hold the stick above you like a wand and make circular motions with your wrist, encasing yourself in a circle of smoke. Visualize yourself being encircled in a ring of protection and divine energy.

3. When you have finished cleansing the space around you (you can determine whether you're finished cleansing by your own intuition or by when the incense burns out), take the candle in your left hand. With your right hand holding the incense, encircle the candle in smoke.

4. Place the incense on a heatproof dish or holder, and with both hands, hold the candle over the incense. Let the smoke rise up to the candle. As the smoke surrounds the candle, visualize it being cleansed, renewed, and purified. You may say a prayer, chant, or speak a few choice words of power, such as "Blessed smoke from sacred earth, give this candle a rebirth."

5. Close your eyes and continue holding the candle over the incense for 2 to 3 minutes, allowing the smoke to cleanse and purify it. When you feel the candle is cleansed and renewed, extinguish the incense, and prepare to move on to the charging process.

# Charging Candles

There's always a purpose or intent behind any spellwork or ritual you perform. When charging a candle, you are simply giving the candle instructions and energetically implementing the task or role it will play in the spellwork. Charging is known as a form of sympathetic magic. You are sending your energy into the candle and telling it what you would like it to accomplish for you. Note that only candles that are specifically used for the main spell or ritual need to be charged. If you are using additional candles, such as tealights, for added energy or ambiance, they do not need to be charged.

To charge most candles used in spellwork, carve them with symbols, names, or other elements. If your candle is contained inside a glass, you may draw these symbols on the glass with a permanent marker. You can also charge candles energetically by visualizing your intent and sending it into the candle.

Follow these steps for a simple and effective charging ritual that you can refer back to for almost every spell in this book:

1. Take your candle, holding it with both hands. Then, close your eyes and visualize what it is you wish the candle to achieve and assist you with. Remember to be specific. Try to imagine the event as if it already happened. If you want health, visualize yourself healed. If you desire love, picture yourself happily with a partner in an everyday scenario. If you want money, visualize a dollar amount or what you wish to obtain with that money. Visualize your desire, and what your life looks like when you get it. Meditate on this wish for a moment, taking as much time as you need.

2. When you have that visual clear in your mind, you're ready to charge the candle. With your eyes still closed and the candle in your hands, replay that scenario in your mind. Take a few breaths and visualize yourself sending those thoughts and intent directly into the candle. Feel the candle getting warm in your hands, filling up with those thoughts and raising those vibrations.

3. At this time, you can carve the candle with sigils, symbols, or words of power. If the candle is intended for someone else, you can write their full name or initials, and perhaps their birthdate and astrological symbol to strengthen the bond. You can also write/draw these symbols onto the glass or write them out on a piece of paper to put beneath the candle (which is also known as making a petition paper).

The images you visualize and the symbols you carve or draw into the candle help structure the spellwork and guide the candle toward its goal. Your energy and visualizations enhance the effectiveness of the candle magic.

# Consecrating Candles

Now that you have given your candle the proper intentions, it is time to consecrate the candle. Consecration is a magical act that designates the tool for ritual use and deems it sacred. Aside from the candle, you can also use this ritual to consecrate any other tools you'd like to use in your spellwork. Just remember that anything you consecrate—a knife or carving tool, wand, matches, or mortar and pestle—should be used for magical purposes only.

The following consecration ritual is specifically for candle magic; however, it can be altered for other tools.

For this consecration ritual, we will be using oil—either an essential oil (a fragrance that corresponds with your intention) or olive oil (which has been used for centuries in antiquity for sacred and magical purposes).

1. Place a dime-size drop of oil in your right hand. With your left hand, grasp the candle at its base. Anoint the oil, starting at the center of the candle and moving upward. Make sure you anoint the entire top half of the candle.

2. When the top half of the candle is completely anointed, reverse the candle by flipping it over, still holding it with your left hand, and anoint the bottom half of the candle. Once again, work from the center and move down, making sure the rest of the candle is completely anointed.

3. After you've completely anointed the candle, grasp the candle with both hands and say, "As above, so below, I call on the spirits I connect with and know." Visualize any spirit guides, deities, ancestors, or archangels you work with to assist in the consecration of your candle. This method incorporates the magical concept of "as above/so below." The idea is that you are sending the intent and energies upward and asking the spirit/angelic realm to bring your desire to the material plane, and then asking the ancestral realm below to offer stability and further assistance in your spellwork.

4. Visualize the candle being imbued with sacred and magical properties, perhaps surrounded by blue flame, white light, or mist.

5. When you've finished calling on your guides for assistance, stare into the candle and say, "This candle is sacred and blessed by the divine; it now wields a magic that matches with mine."

6. Your candle is now consecrated and ready to be put to work.

Although the idea of cleansing, charging, and consecrating may seem tedious, it not only enhances the spellwork—it strengthens your intent and energy, making your spell more likely to succeed and bring about the desired results. At the end of the day, magic is not a simple snap of the fingers or twitch of the nose. Magic takes effort, discipline, and patience—qualities you'll learn and master by doing these rituals.

WITCH TIP

### *Everyday Tools for Drawing*
You can use colored eyeliner pencils to easily draw sigils
and images onto candles.

# Honoring Time

Traditionally, the cleansing, charging, and consecration of candles (let's call the complete practice "the triple Cs") are done in conjunction with the spellwork, or as close as possible to the given time of the ritual. However, life can be hectic, and there are only so many hours in the day. If you find that performing the triple Cs cuts into your spellwork time or makes it inconvenient, then feel free to do it beforehand. For example, I cleanse a candle as soon as I purchase it and will charge and consecrate it as part of my spellwork. Once a candle has been cleansed, there is no need to cleanse it again, unless you are utilizing a candle for multiple purposes and spellwork.

You will find that many spells are intended to be performed on specific days or during lunar phases. When that is the case, I find that it is best to schedule time on a calendar to conduct the spells. Make sure you have all the tools beforehand, and designate some private time so that you can successfully perform the spellwork. If you know that you have a limited amount of time on a specific day (e.g., you'll be home alone for two hours on the full moon), then charge and consecrate the candle the evening before and do the intended spellwork on the proper night. Doing so will divide your spellwork time in half. Make sure that after you prep your candles, you leave them on your altar for spiritual stimulation.

## The Triple Cs

Though used here specifically for candle magic, the cleansing, charging, and consecrating of sacred tools are actually instrumental in all forms of magic. You will find elements of the triple Cs in many traditions including Wicca, Santería, traditional witchcraft, Hoodoo/Voodoo, and Native American shamanism.

# Lighting the Way

Always remember that the candle is a physical representation of your goals, outcomes, and desires. It is important to treat your candle with the proper rituals in order for your spellwork to be successful. Now that you know how to prep your candle, it's time to learn the importance of magical manifestation and the power of properly set intentions.

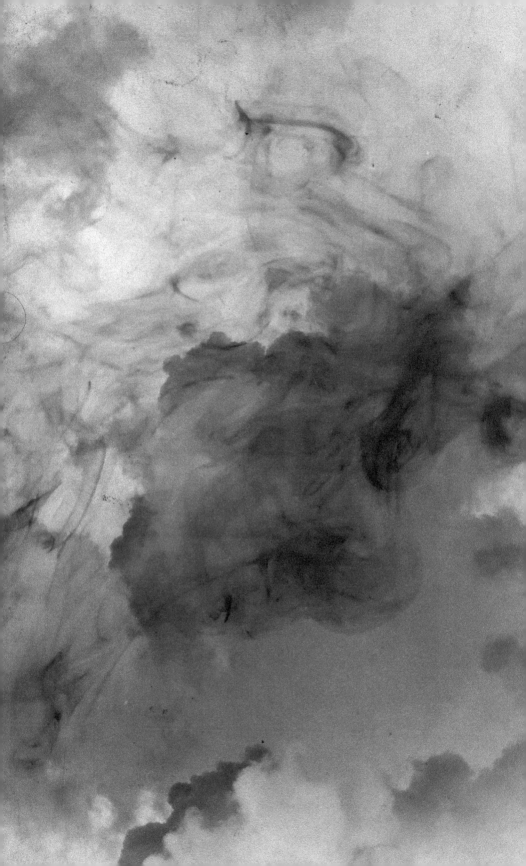

## CHAPTER FIVE

# SETTING INTENTIONS & MASTERING SPELLWORK

No matter what color candle you choose or which oils and herbs you dress your candle with, your spellwork will only be powerful and influential if you have the proper intentions. This chapter will discuss the importance of setting intentions and how to properly and successfully approach spellwork.

# Selecting Spells for Transformation

Within the world of magic, several spells exist for many different purposes. No matter what unique idea, need, or wish may come to mind, there is most certainly a candle that speaks to it, and a spell that can help you execute it. The most popular spells are centered around our most common desires or goals: love, protection, career, health, and abundance. When choosing a spell, first think about what you want to achieve. Do you want a better-paying job? Are you seeking love and companionship? Is your health suffering and in need of healing? Then, seek out the category that best speaks to that need in order to find the most effective spellwork.

## Love

Love spells bring about romance and passion in others as well as yourself. It is important to note that performing love magic is powerful, and the goal should never be to manipulate another person's feelings, free will, or energy. Intentions for love should always be well-thought-out; once clarified, these spells will energetically encourage or give a spiritual "push," so to speak, toward love, passion, and romance.

## Protection

Whether you're seeking safety from harm, an enemy, or a spiritual attack, spells for protection are often necessary when delving into the world of magic. These spells will not only provide spiritual safety from opponents, but also help you erect barriers, wards, and boundaries for your home, loved ones, and yourself.

## Healing

Illness is one of the hardest things to deal with, both physically and emotionally. The healing spells in this book will introduce you to different forms and techniques of healing magic, for emotional, physical, and spiritual ailments. These spells can help heal a current illness as well as protect you and loved ones from future or reoccurring illnesses.

## Prosperity & Abundance

Financial stability is important and can be achieved with a little magical push. Prosperity spells are intended to boost income and fulfill our financial needs. They come in many forms and can assist in a variety of ways. Whether it be obtaining a job, getting paid money you're owed, or finding stability in a new endeavor, there's a spell for that. Add prosperity herbs (rosemary, bay, etc.), coins, dice, and lucky totems (such as a rabbit's foot) to incorporate prosperity and luck into your working. Never ask or plea for prosperity—the best way to yield results is to make a definitive statement that it's going to happen. Crafty spells for luck, fast cash, job promotions, and success reside within these pages.

## Enlightenment

Sometimes we need a little magical fixer-upper to brighten our spirits, and guess what? There's a candle for that! Spells for enlightenment are meant to evoke happiness, fight depression, mend friendships, attract positivity, and offer clarity during stagnant or troubling times. Make sure that you don't manipulate another's feelings magically when performing an enlightenment spell. Some people need to process their feelings and confront them before they can heal or move on. This section includes enchantments to conjure up a little joy, festivity, and positivity in your life.

## Divination, Spirit Communication, Astral Projection & Dreamwork

Practicing magic can also assist in boosting your magic levels! If you're looking to hone divination skills, connect with an ancestor or spirit guide, encourage dreams, gain prophetic wisdom, strengthen spellwork, or work with deities, there are spells to help you achieve just that.

# Magical Manifestations

An intention is a focused desire or objective that is expressed through verbal commands, written words, imagination, or imagery. Setting intentions is a very thoughtful and powerful process, and one that will enhance and inform your candle magic practice each and every time.

Setting intentions and goals is a fundamental part of candle magic; the process begins when a magical practitioner first decides to perform a ritual or spell. It is important to know up front that setting intentions is a powerful process. You must have a clear idea of what you want to achieve and focus intently and purposefully on it. Imagining your desired outcome from the spellwork will enhance not only your powers of manifestation but also your candle magic practice.

Here are a few things to consider when setting an intention before attempting spellwork.

## Meditate on Your Manifestation

Really take some time to think about what you want to happen. What do you want to accomplish? Relax and meditate on your spellwork and imagine your manifestation. What does your outcome look like? Take some time to play around with different scenarios. Look at all the options and personal narratives before settling on a desired goal.

## Set Specific Intentions

Specificity is key! You MUST be incredibly specific when setting intentions, especially when working candle magic and performing spells for goals such as love and money. Sure, saying "I want my boss to give me time off from work" is an intention—but it is so vague, it doesn't guarantee that you'll ever return to work once you get the "time off." An intention such as "I want to get approved for paid time off from work so I can go on vacation" is specific, forward-thinking, and doesn't leave room for error or misinterpretation when doing spellwork. Intentions are truly *that* important—the more specific they are, the more likely you are to achieve a desired outcome.

## Sidestep "Wishes" and Sweeping Goals

Wishes are different from intentions. A wish is weaker, more passive, and essentially a plea. You're giving power to the universe and spirit world and letting them decide, as opposed to making a definitive statement that allows you to create your own fate. A wish might be "I hope my boss likes my interview and I get the job promotion," whereas a stronger intention would be "My boss will acknowledge my hard work, and I will get the job promotion." We may be pleasantly surprised when wishes come true, but we're more likely to arrive at our desired outcome when we set specific, powerful intentions.

## Set Realistic Intentions

Setting intentions is where things get real. We must root our intentions within the realm of the logical, no matter how mundane that may seem. Yes, magic is real, and it can help us obtain things that may seem difficult or out of reach. But the truth is that magic isn't a quick fix to life's problems. Using spellwork to attempt to read your partner's mind is a waste of intentions, spiritual growth, and time. When setting intentions, always think of the logistics beforehand. Is it worth doing spellwork to become CEO of your company if you haven't had any formal training? Or is it a better idea to do spellwork to assist in studying for a business program, or perhaps networking and attracting good partnerships in order to approach your long-term goal of becoming a CEO?

## Set Ethical Intentions

When contemplating desires and outcomes, you must make sure that your intentions are ethical. Remember that if you manipulate the free will of another, you're essentially bringing about something rooted in falsehood. When doing spellwork for yourself or another person, think about the effects it will have. Will anyone get hurt? Will anyone's life be negatively impacted because of it? Your desire should not come at the cost of others, especially if that desire is not organically reciprocated.

When doing love spells, avoid trying to force someone to love you. Instead, focus on spells to boost personal attraction, or to attract attention to yourself.

## Articulate Intentions through Positivity

You must remain hopeful, confident, and positive when making intentions. If you set your intentions with confidence and use positive language when forming them, you're more likely to achieve the desired results and move along a positive path.

In the following list, you will find some sample intentions to help you consider and craft your own before you embark on spellwork:

*(Insert name) will heal quickly and safely.*

*I will get the job I applied for.*

*This year I will travel out of the country and enjoy myself before I begin school again in the fall.*

*I will earn and accumulate the money I need so that I can move next month.*

*I will enter into a committed relationship with someone who loves me unconditionally and is stable financially and emotionally.*

### HOW TO BE INTENTIONAL

Because intentions are one of most important elements of candle magic, you must have a clear intention kept in the forefront of your mind before, during, and after your spellwork. You might also want to repeat your intention out loud. When you put energy and thought into your intentions and goals, you enhance the vibrations of your spell.

### *Formulating Intentions*

When writing or formulating intentions, I find that it's
best to use this simple formula:

- State your desire (try to be as specific as possible)
- Add the time frame you desire to manifest in (if time is an issue or applicable to the scenario)
- Put the desire in present tense using the pronoun "I"
- Try making your intention a command rather than a plea

# Cast the Spell, Light the Flame

Though the second part of this book is dedicated to specific spells, I will first walk you through the general steps of a candle magic spell from start to finish so that you feel prepared. Be sure to refer back to this section if you need assistance on a more difficult spell, or if you decide to modify or write your own spell.

1. Find your intent, meditate on your desire, and focus on what you wish to manifest.

2. Find or formulate the spell you wish to perform.

3. Find the candle type and color best suited to your spellwork.

4. Once you have set your intentions, place your hands over the candle, and send your energy and intentions into it.

5. Follow the directions of the chosen spell step-by-step, and be careful not to rush the process or skip over any details, no matter how big or small.

6. Try finding a carving tool that you use solely for candle magic. This tool can be a nail, sharpened chopstick, pen, or clay carving tool. Make it yours, as this tool will act as a magic wand and conduct your intentions and energy into your candle as you carve it.

7. Safely allow the candle to burn out in a contained environment. If you are unable to allow the candle to burn out on its own, carefully and purposefully extinguish the candle's flame (never blow it out).

8. When the candle has safely burned out or been extinguished, bury the candle if your spell was meant to obtain something. Discard the candle if it was meant to banish something.

## Burn Out & Bury

There is a lot of controversy in the world of candle magic when it comes to blowing out candles. I was taught that blowing out a candle used for spellwork or rituals is offensive to the fire spirits and scatters your intentions, rendering them ineffective. One folk tradition is to snuff out a candle instead of blowing it out. If you want your magic to be successful, you must ensure that the flame goes out on the first try. One of my mentors always pinched out her candles with her fingers as an act of sacrifice to thank the fire for its assistance. I have found it best to extinguish a spellwork flame by snuffing it out or pinching it when you cannot allow the candle to safely burn down on its own. If you find that you have no other alternative but to blow out the candle, simply thank the flame, and reinstate your intention when blowing it out.

Most candles used in magic are meant to burn down completely. If they go out on their own, they should not be relit. If a candle implemented for magic extinguishes by itself, it is an **omen** that the spell you chose to perform cannot help you or that the answer you seek is already determined. In that case, revisit your intention, take a few days to contemplate what it is you truly want, wait at least a week before performing another spell, and discard any contents of the current spellwork away from your property.

When disposing of spellwork, be sure to think of the spell you performed. If the spell was to attract, grow, or obtain something, bury the remnants on the front or back of your property. If you are seeking to banish or remove something, take the remnants of spellwork to a trash bin away from your property. It is always best to wait for the candle to cool down after the completion of the spell, and make sure that all flammable remnants have been properly extinguished.

# Reading the Flame

Keep these signs and indications in mind when you are burning your candle during spellwork:

- **The candle has a hard time lighting.** The type of working you chose will not assist you, and you need to look for another type of spell or ritual.

- **The candle flame splits in two or more flames.** There are other energies that may get involved or intercede with your spellwork and intentions. If this happens, be sure to add an extra layer of protection by doing spiritual fumigation, or create an additional candle for protection.

- **The candle flame is high.** There's a lot of power and energy behind the spell, and a positive outcome.

- **The candle burns very low.** There is a strong opposing force, and a cleansing or banishing may be needed.

- **The flame makes a crackling or a popping sound.** Either the spirits are trying to communicate with you and send you a sign, or there is anticipated communication from the person you might be doing the spellwork for.

- **You attempt to extinguish a candle and it does not go out.** The spirits do not want you to extinguish it. Either let the candle finish burning or wait an additional 13 to 30 minutes before attempting to extinguish it again.

- **The flame goes out while burning.** The spirits cannot help you, and the answer you seek is already determined. The flame can also go out if you unexpectedly get the result before the candle is finished.

# Lighting the Way

Even as a novice to candle magic, you can practice a myriad of spells and focus on and set an infinite number of intentions. Patience is key when it comes to magic; remember to never rush your spellwork and enjoy the process.

In the next part of this book, you'll discover all kinds of spells for candle magic, all with different practices, traditions, and themes. For each spell, I'll list the specific items you need as well as what they symbolize or what energy they bring into the ritual.

Let the sorcery begin!

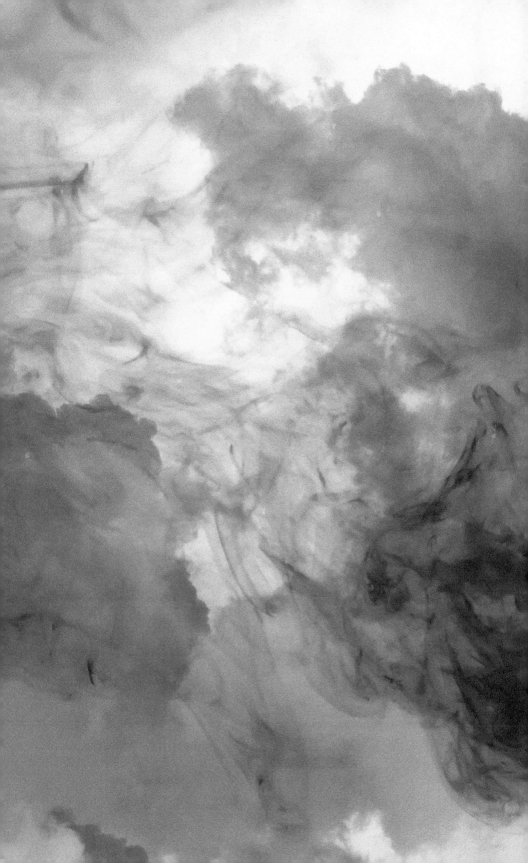

*Part Two*

# TRANSFORMATIVE SPELLS FOR CANDLE MAGIC

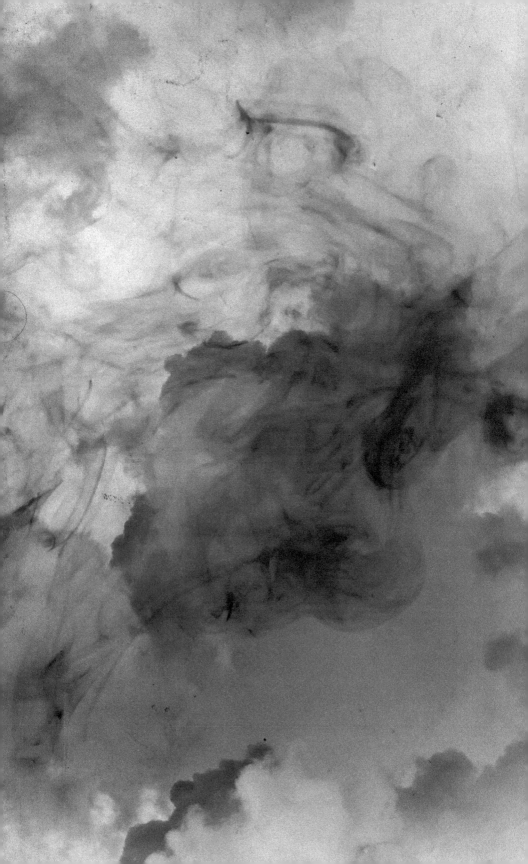

## CHAPTER SIX

# SPELLS FOR LOVE

Love spells have remained the most popular spells throughout history. Love spells both conjure and celebrate love, whether it be carnal or emotional and romantic. They can be used to attract a romantic partner, spark a romance between friends, or awaken passion within yourself. Here you will find several spells that can assist you within the realm of love.

# Welcoming Love, Igniting Love

In this chapter, you will learn how to conjure up that which is most sought after in life—love. Love comes in many forms, and when choosing a love spell, it's important to decide exactly what kind of love you're hoping to acquire: romantic, physical, or platonic. Don't forget to make space for self-love when focusing your intentions and selecting a spell. Before you can start charming the person next door, you must first make sure you have everything you need.

## Common Items Used for Love Spells

**Candle Types:** Pillar, pullout, chime, floating, votive, tealight
**Colors**: Red, pink, white
**Herbs:** Rosemary, jasmine, rose, lavender, damiana
**Oil:** Jasmine, rose, Egyptian musk, vanilla, lavender
**Crystals:** Rose quartz, clear quartz, carnelian, garnet
**Preferred Time:** Love spells are typically best performed in the evening on Fridays and Mondays, during the full moon or waxing moon.

# APHRODITE'S BEAUTY RITUAL

This spell, also known as a glamour spell, is used not only to boost confidence but also to instill within you the beauty, grace, and passion of the ancient goddess Aphrodite herself. It is best to perform this spell in a private room, or when you're alone at home. This spell is traditionally executed in the nude; however, if you wish, you may perform this ritual in your underwear or in shorts and a tank top. For extra-magical potency, perform this spell on a Friday evening during the full moon (if not, then on a Friday evening, or during the next full moon). Give yourself at least two hours to perform and complete the spell. You may wish to burn some frankincense and dress a table with pink cloth, seashells, pearls (real or fake), swan imagery, and rose quartz as an altar for Aphrodite. This ritual can be performed whenever you need a little confidence boost or goddess energy. Once you have performed the spell, continue this visualization when going on dates or pursuing a specific partner.

## MAGICAL ITEMS REQUIRED

Small carving tool (a knife, chopstick, pen, clay carving tool, nail, or pencil)

2 pink chime candles and holders (for romance and love)

Rose oil (for love)

1 red chime candle and holder (for sexuality and lust)

Full-length mirror or large mirror (a vanity or bathroom mirror will do)

Matches or lighter

Strawberry (for aphrodisia and passion)

1 rose quartz (for love and attraction)

## PERFORMING THE SPELL

1. Cleanse, charge, and consecrate your candles to prepare for the spell.

2. Take a bath or shower beforehand to cleanse yourself.

3. Using the carving tool, carve your first name, initials, or first initial and last name on the red chime candle.

4. Carve the word GODDESS on one pink candle and the word APHRODITE on the other pink candle. (If you feel that there's not enough space to write her full name, you may write her Roman name, VENUS.)

5. Using just 1 or 2 drops of rose oil, anoint the three chime candles.

6. Place the chime candles in holders and position them in front of your mirror, with the red candle in the middle flanked on either side by the pink candles. (If using a full-length mirror, the candles should be placed on the floor, but if there is a rug, be sure to place the candles on separate small dishes or plates.)

7. Turn off the lights, so the candles will be your only source of light (or, for your comfort, dim the lights to make it as dark as possible). Make sure you can see your reflection in the mirror.

8. Before lighting the candles, take a moment and imagine the goddess Aphrodite. What does she look like? How does she represent the epitome of beauty to you? What does she, love incarnate, smell like?

9. After envisioning this image in your mind, call Aphrodite forth, either aloud or in your mind.

10. Speak her name before lighting each candle.

11. After you've lit the candles, stare at your reflection in the mirror.

12. If you are wearing clothing, you may remove it at this time.

13. Gaze at your body in the mirror. What do you like about your body? What do you dislike?

14. After looking at your reflection for a moment, let your eyes shift down to look at the candle flames. See how the flames dance and twinkle in the light.

15. Focusing on the flames, let your mind wander. Imagine the flames burning away all your perceived imperfections. Let your focus blur a bit, visualizing the flames surrounding you and filling you with divine light.

16. Let your eyes drift back to your reflection and imagine Aphrodite standing behind your left shoulder.

17. Close your eyes, and visualize Aphrodite fusing with you—her body, soul, and essence joining yours, the two of you becoming one. What does that fusion feel like? Does her presence feel cool, or is it warm? Repeat her name aloud three times: "Aphrodite, Aphrodite, Aphrodite."

18. Open your eyes and stare into the mirror to see your beauty enhanced, your body radiating with light, and your flaws and imperfections smoothed over. See that you are the embodiment of a goddess and feel that truth vibrating within you.

19. While letting your chime candles burn down, take time to sit, rest, or move about your room, still feeling the essence of the goddess within you.

20. When the candles have burned down completely, recline on a bed or couch, eat a strawberry (or a few), and imagine you're consuming a magical aphrodisiac that will fill you with passion and instill within you the powers of a goddess. To enhance and maintain the energy of the spell, anoint a rose quartz with a drop of rose oil. Carry it with you until the next full moon, and then bury it in your backyard or in a potted plant.

# AVALON APPLE LOVE SPELL

Whether you wish to rekindle the flames of a current love
or conjure forth a new one, this spell is sure to do the trick.
Avalon is known as "The Isle of Apples," a sacred place of healing, knowledge, and power. Despite its infamous reputation,
the apple is actually a very potent botanical found in many love
spells throughout history. Perform this spell on a full moon or
a Friday evening. A simple altar with rose quartz, apples, and a
small glass of apple cider or juice can be left out to call on the
assistance of Morgan le Fay, the high priestess, goddess, and
fairy queen of Avalon.

## MAGICAL ITEMS REQUIRED

1 red apple (for passion, sensuality, and vitality)

Small knife or carving tool (if you have someone you wish to use in this
   spell; optional)

Honey (to sweeten the spell)

Cinnamon and clove (for love boost; optional)

2 pink chime candles (for romance)

Offering dish or plate

Matches or lighter

## PERFORMING THE SPELL

1. Hold the apple in both hands, close your eyes, and concentrate.
   Feel the cool temperature of the apple, take a deep breath, and
   imagine the apple radiating warmth starting at its core.

2. Take the blade of your carving tool with your left hand and
   say, "With this blade I pierce the veil, for my heart let love
   set sail."

3. Cut the apple in half horizontally to reveal the pentagram hidden within. Look at both halves of the apple, intently observing the star shape it holds and say, "Like star-crossed lovers in the night, let our light shine till we unite."

4. To sweeten the spell, spread each half of the apple with honey using the same knife. For a boost of love, add cinnamon and/or clove to the apple, if desired.

5. If you have someone in mind who you wish to attract, use the carving tool and carve their initials on one candle and your initials on the other. If you are receptive to new love, skip to step 6.

6. Use each apple half as a base for your candles. Place a chime candle into each half of the apple, using a twisting motion to set it in place.

7. Place both apple halves on the offering dish and draw a circle of honey around each half.

8. Light both candles.

9. Once both candles are lit, take a deep breath. From a safe distance, place a hand above or in front of each flame. Imagine sending your love and light into the candles. Imagine the honey attracting a great love to you, with the candles acting as beacons of light.

10. With your hands still stretched outward in front of the candles, say, "Oh, great lady, Morgan le Fay, I ask you to please send love my way. Like the mighty Excalibur gifted from Avalon's lake, gift me a love whom I'll willingly take."

11. If you can, let the candles burn out completely. (Chime candles typically burn out in 2 to 3 hours.) If you can't leave the candles burning, knock on the table 3 times, thank Morgan le Fay, and snuff (don't blow) the candles out.

12. Repeat the spell again the next day at the same time, until the candles have burned completely.

13. Once the candles are burned down, bury the apples in the earth, preferably near plants associated with love such as roses, lavender, or rosemary to protect your spellwork.

14. After you finish the spell, you may drink some apple cider or juice, or burn an apple-scented candle to add potency to the existing spellwork.

15. During this time, you may go out, start an online dating profile, attend a school reunion, or find a new social group. Who knows who you'll meet?

16. Remember to thank Morgan le Fay and the fairy folk once your spellwork takes action.

# LOVER, COME TO ME SPELL

Whether you have a friendship you want to take to the next level, or someone who caught your eye at work, this spell is intended to attract a specific individual you have in mind for romance. You will be utilizing figure candles, so keep in mind that this spellwork contains very potent magic and energy that you'll be manifesting. Before using this spell, think about whether you really wish to pursue or encourage a romantic relationship with this person. If you simply want a physical relationship or want to seduce someone and are not truly committed to the idea of a monogamous relationship, use red figure candles. It is best to perform this spell on a Friday evening during an even-numbered hour (e.g., 6 p.m., 8 p.m., 10 p.m.) or during a full moon. This spell is intended to be done consecutively—every evening at the same hour until the candles have melted completely.

## MAGICAL ITEMS REQUIRED

2 pink or red figure candles representing the desired relationship (male/female, male/male, female/female, etc.)

Carving tool

4 drops rose essential oil

A black, heatproof ceramic dish

Red thread, preferably thick crafting thread or sewing thread, long enough to wrap around both candles 9 times (for binding and romance)

Matches or lighter

Pink or white cloth (for love encouragement)

## PERFORMING THE SPELL

1. On a Friday evening, take your figure candles and hold one in each hand. Choose which figure candle will represent you, and which one will represent your desired partner. Once you've decided, close your eyes. With the candles still in your hands, envision sending a warm pink stream of energy from your heart down to your arms and hands, and straight into the candles. Meditate on this vision for a moment.

2. Put down the candle that represents you and continue focusing on the candle that represents your desired partner. Think of their personality and physical traits. Send all that energy into the figure candle. Holding that candle in your hands, close your eyes and imagine their essence and personality is being sent through you to the candle itself. Feel it vibrate and pulsate with life and energy.

3. Using the carving tool, carve your full name or initials onto the bottom or backside of the candle representing the person you wish to attract.

4. Next, carve the full name or initials of your desired partner onto the bottom or backside of the candle representing you.

5. Using 2 drops per candle, anoint each figure candle with rose oil.

6. Visualize you and this desired partner bathed in romance and cleansed of anything that might be standing in the way of your love.

7. Place the candles on the dish. Take the thread and begin wrapping it around the 2 candles, making sure they are facing each other. Every time you wrap the thread around the figure candles, say, "With this thread I pull us, heart to heart and skin to skin."

8. After wrapping the thread around the 2 candles 9 times, knot or tuck the thread firmly in place so it doesn't unravel.

9. Light both candles and say, "As passion burns, two become one, let the flames of love burn brighter than the sun."

10. Let the candles burn for 30 minutes to an hour while focusing on your intent. Imagine your future prospects with this person and picture them as your significant other.

11. When finished, snuff (or pinch out with your fingers) the candles, and repeat steps 9 and 10 again tomorrow at the same time.

12. When the candles burn out and melt completely after a few days of this spellwork, look at the images in the wax. Did they take any significant shapes or symbols? (If so, you may want to look them up in a book of symbolism to better understand them. A dictionary of signs and symbols is listed in the Resources section on page 147.)

13. Collect the wax and spell residue, and wrap it in a pink or white cloth.

14. Bury the wrapped cloth, spell residue, and wax in your yard, or in a potted plant on your property.

15. Begin to build your relationship with this desired person, remembering the metaphorical thread you've bound each other with.

# FREYA'S CATNIP PASSION SPICED CANDLE SPELL

Freya is the Norse goddess of love, beauty, and fertility. Cats are sacred to Freya (hence the call for catnip), but that's not where their significance ends; cats also represent sexuality and femininity in many cultures, such as in ancient Egypt. Perform this love spell on a Friday evening, or before or during a romantic encounter that may become physical. The charmed candle enhances the "mood" and gives you the stamina and vigor needed to achieve your passionate goal. This spellwork is intended to be discreet, so it can be done while you're working! Once crafted and charmed, this candle can be used numerous times with multiple people, or just yourself.

## MAGICAL ITEMS REQUIRED

Newspapers, paper towels, or flat dish

1 red pillar candle (for sexuality and passion)

Rose oil (for beauty and love enhancement)

Pinch catnip (for eroticism)

Pinch rosemary (for a magical boost)

Pinch cinnamon (for stamina)

Matches or lighter

## PERFORMING THE SPELL

1.  Prepare your workspace by laying down newspapers, paper towels, or a dish to collect fallen herbs and spices.

2.  Hold the red pillar candle in your hands, close your eyes, and focus on your desire. Imagine your passion, feel your body tingling, and send that energy into the candle.

3. Put a dime-size drop of oil in your hand, and starting at the wick, rub the candle downward toward the base. Envision yourself with your partner, and let your mind drift for a moment, as if in a daydream.

4. After you've anointed the candle, sprinkle a pinch of catnip directly onto it. Turn the candle slowly with your other hand to get the catnip on all sides.

5. As you sprinkle the catnip, say, "Freya, goddess sacred and divine, let this night make my spirit shine."

6. Next, sprinkle a pinch of rosemary on the candle in the same fashion and say, "Rosemary protects my spell, and ensures my outcome turns out well."

7. Then, sprinkle a pinch of cinnamon on the candle in the same fashion and say, "Cinnamon, enchanting and sweet, add to my desire a bit of heat."

8. When you have finishing sprinkling all the herbs and spices, on the candle pick up the newspaper, paper towel, or whatever you used to collect the fallen remnants. Sprinkle whatever has fallen onto the newspaper back onto the candle.

9. Place the candle in a safe spot by your nightstand or in your room.

10. Before your guest arrives, light the candle and say, "Sacred flame, sacred fire, goddess Freya, help me achieve my desire."

11. Let the candle burn until you are done for the evening and ready to go to bed.

12. The candle can be used again until it has completely melted and extinguishes itself.

# CLEOPATRA'S SELF-LOVE MILK BATH MAGIC

Cleopatra, the last pharaoh of Egypt, was known for her charm, intelligence, and beauty. It was also well-known that she was confident and smart and that she captured the hearts and minds of two of the most powerful men of the Roman Empire. This ritual incorporates the ancient Egyptian and Greek custom of ritual **purification**, and also harnesses self-love and strength. Cleopatra was said to soak in fragrant milk and honey baths, which only added to her radiance. Though the ritual calls for a bath, the main focus is the candles utilized in the ritual. Perform this ritual when you are feeling lonely, depleted, unnoticed, depressed, or self-conscious for a powerful boost of self-love.

## MAGICAL ITEMS REQUIRED

1 small piece of paper

Red pen

Kitchen pan

1 cup whole milk (for renewal)

2 tablespoons honey (for attraction)

3 white tealight candles

3 drops frankincense essential oil (for divine blessings and cleansing)

Matches or lighter

## PERFORMING THE SPELL

1. Before starting the ritual, write on a piece of paper with red ink: I AM DIVINE, I AM LOVED, I AM MAGIC.

2. On the stove, combine the milk and honey in the pan, and heat until the honey fully dissolves in the milk, without coming to a boil. (Bubbles will form around the edges and steam will begin to rise.) Let the mixture cool.

3. As the milk and honey mixture cools, prepare a bath in a clean bathtub.

4. After you've prepared your bath to your preferred temperature, arrange the tealights around your tub and in the space around you. The candles can be arranged in front of you or on the sides, whichever way you prefer. Remember to leave enough open, candle-free space so that you can get in and out of the tub safely while the candles burn. Also, make sure to have the petition paper nearby and handy.

5. Add the 3 drops of frankincense oil to the bath and say, "Goddess Isis, divine spirit of love, bless these waters from the heavens above."

6. Next, pour the milk and honey mixture into the bath and say, "Goddess Hathor, I bless this water with your milk. Let my heart be open, and my skin smooth as silk."

7. Light the tealights and step into the bath. Relax for a moment, and imagine the milk and honey purifying your body, and the frankincense clearing away your self-doubt. Imagine yourself incredibly powerful. Think of Cleopatra and what she means to you. What does self-confidence and self-love look and feel like? Purge your feelings of loneliness and pain, and cry if you need to.

8. When you've released your emotions and are ready to move forward, take the petition paper and light it on one of the candle flames.

9.  Watch the paper burn, being careful not to let it burn your fingertips. When it's burned halfway or so, drop the remnants into the tub.

10. Look at the ashes, burnt paper, and candles. Staring at the candles, say positive affirmations about yourself like "I am smart; I am kind; I am beautiful."

11. Take some time to soak in the bath. Gently rub yourself with a damp washcloth, and fill yourself with loving energy. Think of happier times.

12. When you feel that you've soaked long enough, extinguish the tealights with water from your bath.

13. Bury the tealights outdoors.

14. After your bath, wear elements of gold to invoke the energy of the candles and the ancient powers you harnessed during the ritual.

15. Repeat this ritual whenever necessary.

# C'EST L'AMOUR VOODOO LOVE CONJURE

Voodoo, specifically New Orleans Voodoo, is a blend of religious and magical elements that incorporate African, Native American, European, and Catholic beliefs. This spell is intended to either attract the person you love or encourage a new romance. This simple spell is most effective when the moon is either full or waxing. You may perform this spell outside beneath the moon, or at a window where the moon is visible. The inspiration for this spell comes from Denise Alvarado's *Voodoo Hoodoo Spellbook.*

## MAGICAL ITEMS REQUIRED

1 red pen

1 piece of paper

1 pink chime candle (for love and romance)

Carving tool

1 drop honeysuckle oil (for love attraction)

Matches or lighter

## PERFORMING THE SPELL

1. Write who or what you want in red ink on the paper.

2. Take a pink chime candle and engrave a heart into it using the carving tool.

3. Anoint the candle from wick to base with a drop of honeysuckle oil.

4. If you're indoors, place the candle on your windowsill with the heart facing the window, so that the moon may charge it.

5. Place the piece of petition paper beneath the candle's base.

6. Place the bottle of honeysuckle oil next to the candle.

7. Light the candle and say, "Sacred powers from above, please attract the one I love."

8. Let the candle burn down completely (about 1 to 2 hours).

9. Collect the remaining wax and petition paper and bury them near your property. Visualize that you are planting a seed, and a new love will bloom and grow from the buried remnants.

10. Wear a dab of honeysuckle behind your ears from the bottle you charged in the moonlight whenever you go out to meet people.

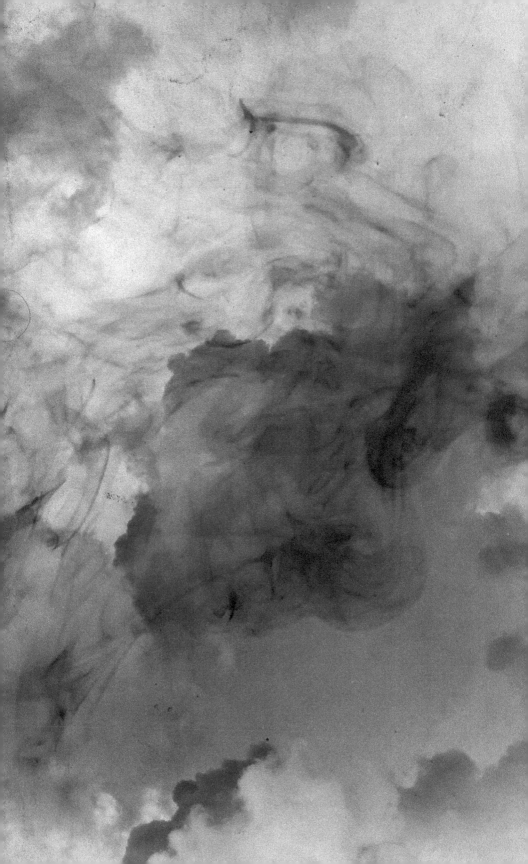

CHAPTER SEVEN

# SPELLS FOR HEALING

Whether you need to heal a broken heart, bounce
back from an injury, or recover from an illness,
the following spells will help you provide healing
benefits and vibrations to yourself and those
you love and care for.

# Seeking Healing, Providing Healing

It is important to note that the purpose of healing spells is not simply to fix or eradicate injury or illness but to sooth and mend as well. Healing comes in many forms and guises.

When doing healing spells for others, make sure you check in with yourself and meditate on these questions: Would they mind you doing spellwork for them? Would your spellwork interfere with their free will? If you feel comfortable with your practice, ask permission from the person you wish to do spellwork for.

## Common Items Used for Healing Spells

**Colors:** White, blue, black
**Herbs:** Carnelian, quartz, labradorite, hematite, amethyst, rose quartz
**Oil:** Eucalyptus, rosemary, olive oil, bergamot
**Preferred Time:** Mondays, Sundays, full and waning moon

# SACRED PILLAR OF WELLNESS

This simple spell uses a pillar, pullout, or novena candle, and is meant to ward off illness. A wellness spell like this one is great if you have an upcoming event you don't want to miss, have recently been around someone who was ill, or just want more energy. It's best to perform this spell during a waning moon.

## MAGICAL ITEMS REQUIRED

1 white pillar candle (for healing)

1 dime-size drop olive oil (for purification)

1 blue marker (or an eyeliner pencil if you're using a pillar candle on a heatproof dish without glass)

Matches or lighter

## PERFORMING THE SPELL

1. Cleanse, charge, and consecrate your candle to prepare for the spell.

2. If you are using a novena candle, skip to step 3. If not, pour a dime-size drop of olive oil into your palm and anoint the candle from base to wick in a pulling motion. Imagine you're pushing out any traces of illness that might be hanging around you or within you (this illness could be physical or mental) and purging yourself of all sickness and negative energy.

3. Using the blue marker, write the words *NULLUM ME NOCEBIT* ("nothing will harm me") anywhere on the candle.

4. Take a moment to visualize yourself shielded by a blue flame.

5. Light the candle and say aloud, "Nothing will harm me."

6. Let the candle burn down completely.

7. When the candle has burned down, bury the remnants in your yard (if the candle was in a glass, recycle that piece).

# APOLLO'S HEALING FLAME

Apollo is the ancient Greek god of healing as well as the god of prophecy, music, and the sun. This spell uses sympathetic magic to create physical representations of your illnesses and symptoms, and then burns them up in the sacred flame. To enhance your spellwork, you can create an altar to Apollo using the color gold and decorate it with sun and raven/crow imagery. This spell should be performed on a Sunday.

## MAGICAL ITEMS REQUIRED

1 white votive candle (for healing)

Dime-size drop olive oil (for purification)

Heatproof dish

1 red marker

3 small pieces of paper

Matches or lighter

## PERFORMING THE SPELL

1. Anoint the votive candle with a dime-size drop of olive oil. Meanwhile, visualize a bright light surrounding you, and the warmth of the sun shining down on you.

2. Place the anointed votive candle on the dish.

3. Think about what ails you. Try to visualize your symptoms and how they make you feel.

4. Using the red marker, write down your symptoms on the pieces of paper. If you have a specific illness or diagnosis, write that on one piece of paper and your symptoms on the other two. If you don't have a diagnosis, write down your symptoms on all 3 pieces of paper.

5.  Draw 9 lines across each piece of paper, making sure you cross through the words you've written.

6.  Light the candle and stare at the flame. Take a deep breath and say, "Lord Apollo, god of light, heal me and destroy my plight."

7.  Take the first piece of paper and burn it in the candle flames while saying, "Scorch my illness, let me heal, in this flame, no pain I'll feel."

8.  Take the second piece of paper and burn it in the candle flame while saying, "My ailments die in smoke and flame, I purge this sickness in Apollo's name."

9.  Take the third paper, hold it to your chest, take a breath, and envision your pains, ailments, sickness, and any feelings of toxicity burning away in the flames. Imagine the paper in your hand is all that remains of the sickness. Burn the paper in the flames and say, "My thread of fate is mighty and strong, Apollo, heal what's broken and wrong."

10. After you've burned the last of the papers, let the candle burn out completely. Take any wax remnants or ashes and flush them down your toilet or garbage disposal with running water. Meanwhile, envision yourself completely healed.

11. Perform this spell biweekly if needed.

# HEALING CANDLE OF MARIE LAVEAU

This spell comes from my friend, mentor, and the Voodoo queen of New Orleans, Bloody Mary! A miraculous healer in New Orleans during the 19th century plagues, Marie Laveau is now seen as a relentless spirit mother; her tomb remains a shrine to people from all over the word who travel to New Orleans to seek her divine intervention. In this healing candle spell, you are evoking the great Voodoo queen of New Orleans to assist in the magical working. This spell can be performed for someone else's health, but can be altered to suite your own needs as well. Perform this spell to recover from both physical and mental ailments. Perform on a Monday evening during a waning moon.

When practicing any New Orleans Voodoo, remember to tithe (give a tenth of your income) to a charity or church after the spell has been performed to pay for the work in the spirit world. Remember to imbue your candle with prayer or song and strong visualization of the desired outcome.

## MAGICAL ITEMS REQUIRED

Cornmeal (for earth, growth, and substance)

White cloth (for purification)

Candleholder

Carving tool, pen, or bone knife

Blue or white pullout candles

Pen or pencil

Rum (for offering and libation)

Elderberry syrup or tea (for health)

Holy water or rainwater (for renewal)

Matches or lighter

Rattle, bells, or drum

Picture of client (or the presence of the actual client)

Notebook

## PERFORMING THE SPELL

1. Create a sacred, cleansed area for your altar space.

2. Make an X out of cornmeal at the base of the working altar.

3. Put a white cloth over the X.

4. Put a safe candleholder on top of that cloth.

5. In Voodoo, always dedicate the candle to a particular loa (spirit) or saint—in this case, Marie Laveau.

6. Using the carving tool, carve an X, preferably near the center, on a blue or white candle. (This carving is a simple Voodoo cosmogram, and the symbol for crossroads.)

7. Write the name "Marie Laveau" on the candle in pen or pencil.

8. Write the client/patient name or initials on the candle. (Write the initials only if the client is present. Write their full name and use a photo if working remotely.)

9. Dress the candle, rubbing with the rum first, then the elderberry.

10. Sprinkle or pour 3 drops of holy water on your altar and on the floor or ground, depending on your setup and location.

11. Knock 3 times on the table and say, "Open the gates, St. Peter, *passe porte!* May I open the way, Papa Legba? Let your children pass. *Yo La li Mamzelle* Marie; Marie Laveau, oh spirit mother of healing touch, I call upon you; *Yo La li Mamzelle* Marie!"

12. Introduce yourself, state your intention, and your plea for help.

13. Light the candle.

14. Shake the rattle, ring the bells, or beat the drum 3 times. Rattle, ring, or drum 3 times, again and again, until you feel the energy shift.

15. Rub your hands together in the heat of the flame, and have your client do the same if they are with you for the spellwork.

16. Take the candleholder with the lit candle inside of it to the client, or to the picture of the client.

17. Trace the candlelight all around the patient's/client's body or picture. (If you are with the client in person, pick up their feet, one by one, to trace under their feet.)

18. Put the candle back.

19. Sit in silence with the client, or observe a moment of silence if working remotely. Have a notebook handy to write down any messages or advice that you receive from Marie Laveau.

20. Meditate as you visualize Voodoo Queen Marie Laveau stepping in and spiritually touching your client.

21. Let the candle burn for about 20 minutes.

22. Extinguish the candle and relight it for 15 to 20 minutes each day over the course of 3 days. You may then give the candle to the person intended to receive the healing to have them complete the process of burning the candle down or do that for them if they can't or won't, but it is better if they participate.

23. Close the magical working by clapping 3 times.

24. Thank the spirit for their help.

25. Release the spirit while asking for healing to continue and protection to remain.

26. Say, "*Ayibobo.*"

# MENTAL HEALTH MAGIC

I crafted this healing spell during my high school days while dealing with stress and anxiety. It's a relatively simple spell that combines the power of candle magic with the energetic healing forces of music and meditation. Perform this spell in your room, or a dark space where you can be alone but still feel safe. Do this spell on a Sunday evening, or whenever you feel overwhelmed, anxious, or in a negative headspace.

## MAGICAL ITEMS REQUIRED

A space where you can be alone

Frankincense or other purification herbs (palo santo, sage, sweetgrass, or rosemary, for cleansing)

Song playlist

6 white chime candles (for healing)

Speakers or headphones

Matches or lighter

## PERFORMING THE SPELL

1. Cleanse your room or space with frankincense or other purification herbs of your choice (palo santo, sage, sweetgrass, or rosemary).

2. Create a playlist. First, choose 3 songs that represent what you're currently feeling, or the lowest you've felt. Then, choose 3 songs that represent the happiest you've ever been, or songs that uplift you.

3. Space out the 6 chimes around you on the floor, making sure they're within reach but also at a safe distance so that you can lie down.

4. Light all 6 candles.

5. Turn out the lights in the room so that the space is illuminated by candlelight only.

6. When you're ready, play the first song on your playlist, the one that represents your fears, depression, and hurt. Close your eyes, and as the song plays, feel the emotions that stir within you. The longer the song plays, the more those feelings rise up (as if a tea kettle is boiling). Breathe through your emotions.

7. When the song has finished playing, immediately sit up, look at a candle, and blow it out. Imagine you're blowing out all of those feelings and emotions and sending them away.

8. Returning to a relaxed position, continue on to the second song. Repeat steps 6 and 7.

9. After you've blown out the candle on the third and last song of the cycle of sad songs, take a minute to breathe.

10. Imagine yourself purged of the sorrow and pain and visualize yourself hollow but peaceful inside.

11. Return to your relaxed position and play the first upbeat song on the playlist. This song represents your wants, desires, and dreams.

12. When the song has finished, sit up and stare into the candle flame. But this time, don't blow the candle out—keep the good vibes going.

13. Repeat steps 11 and 12.

14. As you begin to listen to the last song, imagine the happiest you've ever been. Think of a memory that makes you smile, and events yet to come that make you happy.

15. When you've finished, take the 3 candles you blew out, and quickly dispose of them in the trash. Imagine yourself tossing out the bad feelings and vibes.

16. Snuff out the remaining chime candles and save them. These candles have been charged with your longings, desires, and happy memories, and can be lit whenever you wish to invoke those feelings again.

# HERA'S HEALING HEARTBREAK SPELL

Hera, the wife of Zeus and ancient Greek goddess of marriage, constantly battles with her husband and his unfaithful transgressions throughout mythology. Even though Hera suffered many betrayals, she still managed to maintain her composure and heal from hurt. As a goddess, she looks after those who have been heartbroken and nurtures those who need a little pick-me-up. Perform this spell on a Sunday or waning moon. To amplify your spellwork, decorate an altar with green or purple cloth, and peacock feathers or imagery of peacocks, which are sacred to Hera. This spell can be done right before bed following a breakup, the arrival of unfortunate news, the end of a friendship, a personal loss, or anytime you feel lonely.

## MAGICAL ITEMS REQUIRED

1 blue chime candle (for healing)

Carving tool

Candleholder

Matches or lighter

Journal or notebook

Red pen

1 fresh or dried rosemary sprig (for protection, enchantment boost)

1 drop lavender oil (for relaxation and peace)

## PERFORMING THE SPELL

1. A few hours before bedtime, take a blue chime candle and, using the carving utensil, carve the words *FORTIS IN ARDUIS* ("Strong in difficult situations") into the side of the candle.

2. Place the candle on a holder by your nightstand and light the candle. In your mind or out loud, ask for healing blessings and for the pain and heartache that you're feeling to be removed.

3. Take your journal or notebook and draw a circle. Within the circle, draw a heart, and within the heart, write the word HEAL.

4. Tear out the page and place it on your nightstand. Then, take your candle and carefully drip the wax around the circle you drew.

5. Place the candle on top of the paper, in the center of the drawn circle.

6. Turn off any remaining lights, get the rosemary sprig, and return to your bed. As you clutch the rosemary sprig, stare at the candle flame and say, "Lady Hera, I ask you to heal my heart that's broken, and in return I give you this token."

7. Place the rosemary under your pillow.

8. As the candle burns down, imagine it's burning away the heartbreak and pain.

9. When the candle has burned out completely, place a drop of lavender oil on your fingertips and rub your temples.

10. Go to bed. Try to relax and not think of the situation.

11. In the morning, collect the spell remnants (the wax and paper). Crumple up the remnants and toss them into the trash or take them to a garbage can located away from your property.

12. Keep the rosemary sprig and place it on your altar as a reminder of Hera's protection. After a month, bury the sprig in your yard to welcome new feelings of love.

# HECATE'S HEALING VIGIL RITUAL

Hecate is one of the most famous goddesses today in Paganism and modern witchcraft. She is widely recognized as a lunar goddess and queen of witches, but like her triple goddess nature, she is constantly evolving and changing. Originally, she was a Greek Titan and possessed the power of life and death. She controls the earth, underworld, sea, and moon. She is the matron of herbalists and midwives. Those in need of healing would petition Hecate, or journey to her sacred garden on the isle of Colchis to receive a blessing by one of her priestesses. This ritual is intended to be used as a last resort, such as when no medical answer or treatment is available. You can also use this ritual to ask for a diagnosis or understanding of what is going on with you or a loved one. Perform this spell on the evening of a dark moon, or on a Monday night. Prepare an altar by setting a table with black cloth, and decorate it with pomegranates and apples as well as figures, pictures, and imagery of Hecate's sacred creatures—dogs, snakes, and dragons. This ritual is done consecutively for nine days.

## MAGICAL ITEMS REQUIRED

Death card (for renewal) and moon card from a tarot deck

1 black novena or seven-knob candle (for Hecate)

Carving tool

1 drop olive oil (for purification)

Heatproof dish

Matches or lighter

## PERFORMING THE SPELL

1. After you set up your altar, remove the death and moon cards from your tarot deck.

2. Hold the death card in your hand and stare at the imagery; what does the art reveal to you? The death card is not an indication of an ending but of a transformation. Hold the card in your hand and speak to it. Vocalize who you wish to be healed and what their symptoms are.

3. Place the death card on the table and pick up the moon card. Stare at the picture on the card and imagine the moon is the goddess Hecate herself. The moon represents mystery and the unknown. As you stare at the card, speak aloud and ask that a proper prognosis be revealed as well as a cure or treatment.

4. Place the moon card back on the table and pick up the black candle in both hands. With your eyes closed and holding the candle in both hands, speak the name of the person you are doing the working for aloud 3 times.

5. Using the carving tool, carve the name HECATE on the top of the candle and the person's name on the bottom of the candle.

6. Pour a dime-size amount of olive oil in your left hand and anoint the candle starting from the base, working your way to the top, toward the wick.

7. Place the candle on the dish, and place it behind the tarot cards you previously charged.

8. Light the candles with the match and say aloud or internally, "I strike the match and light the flame; mighty Hecate, I call your name. Reveal to me what's been concealed, help me cure, protect, and shield."

9. Place the used match on the dish next to the candle and let the candle burn for 13 to 30 minutes. Then snuff the candles with your fingers.

10. Relight the candle every evening for 13 to 30 minutes for 9 consecutive days or until the candle is completely burned out and extinguished by itself.

11. If any remaining wax is left, look to see if specific images stand out. Look up their symbolism in the recommended dictionary of signs and symbols mentioned in the Resources section (page 147).

12. Dispose of any remaining wax in a trash receptacle away from your property.

13. Keep the tarot cards you used for the ritual on your dresser or desk until you or the person you've conducted the spell for receives proper treatment or an accurate diagnosis.

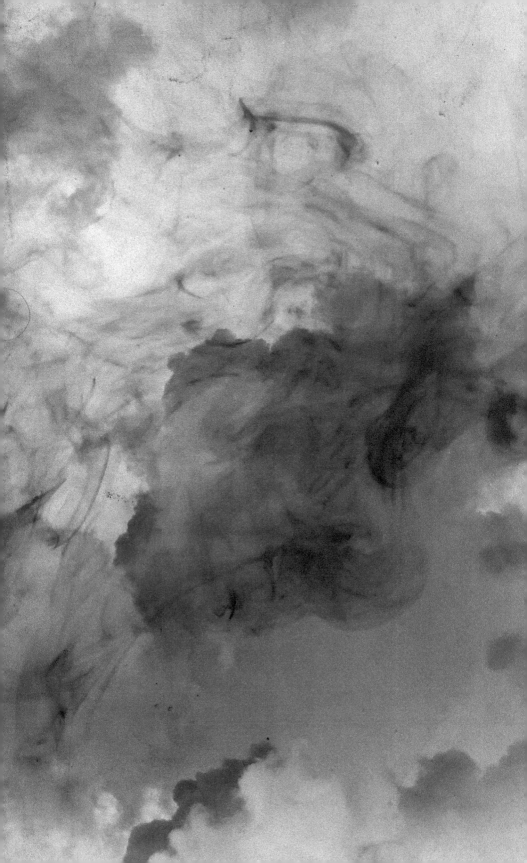

CHAPTER EIGHT

# SPELLS FOR PROTECTION

Second only to love, protection is one of the most sought-after and popular spell categories. Protection spells shield you from negative forces, both physical and supernatural. In this chapter, you will find an assortment of spells geared to protect you from gossip, false friends, trickster spirits, and negative energy that might be hanging around.

# Invoking Protection, Enacting Protection

Everyone needs protection at some point, and there's nothing like being protected magically. These spells will not only deter enemies and fend off bad **juju**, but also protect you from supernatural specters.

## Common Items Used for Protection Spells

**Candles:** Pillar, pullout, novena, tealight
**Color:** Black, white
**Herbs:** Rosemary, black peppercorn, red pepper flakes, cayenne pepper
**Oils:** Frankincense, myrrh, rosemary
**Stones:** Clear quartz, smoky quartz, hematite, tiger's-eye, black tourmaline
**Preferred Time:** Waning moon, Monday, Tuesday

# KEMETIC FLAME
# OF PROTECTION

The ancient Egyptians were masters of sorce
is adapted from one found in an ancient papyru
spell originally called for the use of a lamp, as candles were
not utilized in magic until much later; this modern take uses a
pullout candle instead. This simple spell can also be performed
before or during any magic or spellwork for protection against
outside influences. You will need to let this candle burn down
completely, which will take several days. Perform this spell on a
Tuesday, or whenever you feel in need of protection.

## MAGICAL ITEMS REQUIRED

1 black pullout candle (for banishing)

Carving tool

1 drop frankincense oil (for protection)

Pinch myrrh resin (for cleansing)

Pinch dried rosemary (for enchantment boost)

Matches (sulfur for protection)

## PERFORMING THE SPELL

1. Take the black pullout candle in both hands. Close your eyes,
   inhale, and gently blow onto the candle. As you blow, visualize
   yourself filling the candle with protective energy.

2. Using the carving tool, carve the eye of Ra into the candle wax.
   Be careful not to carve too deep.

Pour a dime-size drop of frankincense oil into your hand. Starting at the base of the candle, rub the oil up toward the wick. Visualize yourself pushing out any bad energy or toxicity that may be hanging around you.

4. Drop a pinch of myrrh resin into the bottom of the candle-holder glass, then add a pinch of rosemary.

5. Place the candle back into the glass, hold it in both hands, and say, "Father Sun, hear my plea, let your watchful eye protect me."

6. Strike and light a match. As you light the candle with the match, say, "I strike the match, I say Ra's name, and I'm protected by his sacred flame."

7. Meditate with the candle for 10 to 15 minutes. As you stare at the candle, visualize yourself being surrounded and protected by its flames.

8. When the candle has burned out completely, look at the glass to see if there's any soot. How did the candle burn? How long did it take to finish? (See page 49 for tips on reading your own candle.)

9. Recycle the glass after use.

# BITCH BE GONE

We've all had that one person (okay, maybe more than one) in our lives—the one we encounter and then quickly realize, this bitch needs to go! If you've been wronged or need to get rid of someone who has slighted you, then this protective candle spell will help. It packs some mighty magic and gives a nice little push out the door for someone who may have crossed boundaries, overstayed their welcome, or caused trouble. This spell is quick to perform and works quickly! Perform it on a waning moon.

## MAGICAL ITEMS REQUIRED

Carving tool

Sewing pin or needle

1 black chime candle (for banishing)

Small ceramic dish (preferably black)

Pinch cayenne pepper (for banishing and speeding up the process)

Pinch crushed black pepper (for banishing)

Pinch salt (for protection)

Matches or lighter

Black cloth or rag

## PERFORMING THE SPELL

1. Think of the person you wish to remove from your life. Using the carving tool, carve their name or initials into the candle.

2. Take a sewing pin or needle and pierce through the candle, taking care not to break the candle in half. (If you can't get the needle all the way through, halfway is fine.)

3. As you pierce the candle say, "(Insert name), you've done me wrong, and now I say, bitch, move along."

4. Place the candle on the dish. (You will need to melt the bottom of the candle a little to help it stand on the dish.)

5. Take a pinch of the cayenne pepper and sprinkle it around the candle in a circular motion within the dish.

6. Repeat step 5 using the black pepper and salt.

7. After you've sprinkled the circle of salt around the candle, say, "Bitch be gone, that's what I say. Yes, bitch be gone, please go away."

8. Light the candle. As it burns, visualize the person the spell is for. Visualize all their features and imagine them slowly disappearing, almost as if they're becoming translucent, until suddenly they vanish.

9. Let the candle burn until the pin falls out or drops. After the pin falls out, extinguish the candle by snuffing it out.

10. Collect the candle and herbs from the dish into a black piece of cloth, fold it up, and secure it with the pin.

11. Take the bundled herbs and candle to a trash far away from your property. Toss the bundle into the trash and say, "Bitch be gone."

12. Block the toxic person on social media and take the proper steps to distance yourself from them.

13. You may wish to continue burning a black chime candle once a week until the person has been fully removed from your life. Remember, don't engage.

# BAD VIBES BANISHMENT

Let's face it: Sometimes people are in a mood! The last thing we want is another person's negative energy hanging around us, especially when it's in our personal space or home. This ritual is the perfect way to cleanse a home from bad vibes, residual energies of negative people, or energy that might be hanging around from a previous owner or inhabitant. This spell is effective, efficient, and only requires salt, tealights, matches, and the powers within you! Perform this spell anytime you suddenly feel bad vibes, or when the energy in your home seems off. You can also perform this spell when you first move into a new place.

## MAGICAL ITEMS REQUIRED

4 white tealight candles (for cleansing)

4 matches (for banishing)

Salt (for protection)

## PERFORMING THE SPELL

1. Arrange the 4 tealights in the 4 corners of your living space, preferably the living room.

2. Starting at the back of the house, in the area farthest away from the front entrance to your home, choose a corner, light a tealight, and say, "I strike the match, I light the flame. Banish bad vibes within this plane." Light the candle and leave the used match next to the tealight.

3. Sprinkle a pinch of salt around the tealight and say, "Sulfur and salt absorb what's bad, dry up what's painful, negative, and sad."

4. Repeat steps 2 and 3 for the remaining corners.

5. After you've lit all 4 corners and sprinkled the salt, return to the center of the room. Sit on the floor with your legs crossed, close your eyes, and take a few deep breaths. Visualize the space around you becoming super bright and being enveloped in a white light. Imagine this light eradicating all the heavy, negative energy.

6. When you feel that the space has been cleansed, collect the tealights and matches, and toss them in a garbage away from your property.

7. You may continue cleansing the house with any other rituals or tools you like, but do this spell first to absorb and trap the negative energies that may be lingering.

# HEX BREAKER

Are you having a string of bad luck? Do you feel off? F
upset anyone who might've thrown a hex on you? It's important to know that not all hexes and curses are cast with spells.
Anger, jealousy, and rage can put out a lot of potent energy,
especially when it's directed at someone specific. This spell is a
great way to banish any bad juju hanging around. Use this spell
whenever you feel drained or know that someone is wishing ill
will on you. The best time to cast this spell is during the waning
moon, or on a Thursday at 9 p.m. Be sure to decorate an altar
with a black cloth and perform the spell under dim lighting.

## MAGICAL ITEMS REQUIRED

1 black votive candle

Carving tool

Olive oil

Dish or bowl (preferably black)

9 black peppercorns

Salt

Matches

Black cloth bag (optional)

## PERFORMING THE SPELL

1. Holding the unlit black votive candle in your hand, imagine
   all the unfortunate events or weird turns of luck that have
   befallen you as of late. Close your eyes, take a deep breath, and
   blow onto the candle. Repeat the words, "I give you life with
   this enchanter's breath."

2. Using the carving tool, carve an equal-armed cross into the
   candle. As you carve, imagine yourself encircled in a protective blue flame.

3. Anoint the votive with a dab of olive oil, encircling the candle counterclockwise and ensuring that the entire candle is anointed.

4. Place the votive candle on the dish and take the 9 peppercorns in your left hand.

5. With your right hand, pick up a peppercorn and say, "Whatever has been thrown at me, I break it off, so mote it be," and place the peppercorn on the dish around the candle. Repeat this process until all the peppercorns surround the candle in a circle.

6. Pour some salt into your left hand. Clasp this hand into a fist and envision the salt absorbing all your negativity. With your right hand, take the salt and sprinkle it around the candle in a clockwise motion.

7. Hold the matches in your left hand and whisper, "Sacred sulfur, from this match, protect me from negativity I might catch."

8. Strike the match and light the candle, leaving the match as an offering on the dish.

9. If you can, let the candle burn down completely. If not, let the candle burn for an hour and then snuff it out and sprinkle it with salt.

10. When the candle has burned out completely, look at any shapes the wax may have left behind. You can read about these shapes or symbols to gauge what might have brought about this hex. If no wax was left behind, the spell was a complete success.

11. You can keep the peppercorns and any salt residue in a small black cloth bag for a protection charm. Alternatively, flush the peppercorns and salt down the toilet or sink while focusing on banishing the bad luck.

# PYTHIA'S PURIFICATION & PROTECTION

The Pythia was the oracle of Delphi in ancient Greece. In antiquity, people from all around used to make a pilgrimage to consult the Pythia and ask for a prophecy. The oracle was also a priestess dedicated to Apollo, the god of healing, the arts, the sun, and prophecy. This ritual is meant to be done after spellwork or divination. The intention is not only to cleanse and purify yourself but also to protect yourself from outside forces that may intervene when casting a spell or doing divination (tarot, scrying, mediumship, or intuitive readings). This ritual can be done at any time and should be implemented after spellwork, especially if the reading or spellwork is for another person. You never want to have the intentions, feelings, or energies of others clinging to you. For this purifying and pro-tecting ritual, create an altar space of pure white with elements of gold and amethyst or smoky quartz to cleanse your psychic energy and third eye.

## MAGICAL ITEMS REQUIRED

1 black chime candle (for banishing)

Olive oil (for purification)

2 white chime candles (for protection)

3 drops rosemary essential oil (for enchantment boost and protection)

1 drop lavender essential oil (for purification; optional)

Bowl of water

Gold marker

3 bay leaves (for protection, sacred to Apollo)

Matches or lighter

## PERFORMING THE SPELL

1. After you've performed your spellwork or divination, anoint the black candle with a dime-size amount of olive oil and a white candle with rosemary oil. Anoint the other white candle with lavender oil, if desired. Say aloud or to yourself, "Lord Apollo, god of light, thank you for your gift of sight."

2. Arrange the candles so that the black candle is in the middle, flanked by the 2 white candles.

3. Place the bowl of water in front of the 3 candles.

4. Using the gold marker, write APOLLO on the first bay leaf. Write PYTHIA on the second and ARTEMIS on the third. When you're done writing the names on the leaves, place them off to the side.

5. Strike a match and light the candles, beginning with the white chime candle on the left side. Use one match for each candle; after each candle is lit, drop the match into the bowl of water in front of you.

6. After all 3 candles are lit, take the bay leaf that says APOLLO and light it with the flame of the candle that you lit first.

7. As you light the bay leaf, say, "Apollo, I speak your sacred name, please bless me with the light of this flame." Let the bay leaf burn as much as you can without burning yourself, and then drop the burning leaf into the bowl of water.

8. Take the second bay leaf, which says PYTHIA, and burn it on the other white chime candle. As you light the bay leaf, say, "Pythia, spirit of prophecy, my working is finished, please protect me." Let the leaf burn as much as possible, then drop it into the bowl of water.

9. Take the final leaf, which says ARTEMIS, burn it in the flame of the black candle, and say, "Artemis, goddess of moon and night, I petition protection with this sacred rite." Let the leaf burn as much as possible, then drop it into the bowl of water.

10. When you've dropped the last leaf into the water, hold your hands a safe distance above the flames, feeling the heat rising up. Close your eyes for a moment and visualize the flames burning away the excess energy and any lingering muck (negativity, anger, bad vibes, or feelings) from the spellwork or reading you did previously.

11. Open your eyes, stare at the burning candles, and say, "Protect my magic, protect my sight, protect me from that which is not light."

12. Wash your hands in the bowl of water and sprinkle some water on your head and the back of your neck.

13. Let the candles burn down completely (this should take about 1 to 3 hours). Use this time to relax and meditate.

14. When the candles have burned out, drop the remnants into the bowl of water, and flush them down the toilet or put them in the garbage disposal with running water. (Back in antiquity, banishing spells were disposed of in lakes or rivers, but flushing the remnants is just as good.)

# CARIBBEAN COCONUT CLEANSING CANDLE

This traditional Obeah-style spell was shared by a beloved friend from Trinidad. Obeah is an Afro-Caribbean spiritual, healing, and magical folk practice used in the Bahamas, Caribbean, Jamaica, Trinidad, and the Virgin Islands. In this cleansing spell, the candle is housed in a coconut to symbolize strength and protection, and is buried after the spellwork is complete. This spell calls on your ancestors (known and unknown) and is intended to cleanse a space and help ward off bad spirits, negative energy, and unwanted guests. Perform this spell on an evening during the waning moon and prepare an altar table with white linens.

## MAGICAL ITEMS REQUIRED

3 white votive candles (for purification)

Dime-size drop coconut oil (for renewal)

½ coconut shell (for the earth and protection)

3 drops patchouli essential oil (for spiritual enhancement)

1 drop myrrh oil (for divine blessings)

Matches (for banishing)

## PERFORMING THE SPELL

1. Begin by anointing the 3 white votives with a dime-size drop of coconut oil. Secure the 3 candles inside the coconut half.

2. Place one drop of patchouli oil on each votive. You may speak your intention, or any other words of power, at this time.

3. Place a drop of myrrh oil in between each of the 3 candles and say, "Divine ancestors, hear my plea, make this place a sacred space."

4. Light the candles with the matches (one match per candle) and place the burned-out matches inside the coconut.

5. As the candles burn, visualize them emitting a white light that encompasses the entire space.

6. Hold your hands above the candles while keeping a safe distance. Feel the heat of the flames rising up to your palms. Visualize yourself being purified and purged of any toxicity that may be lingering around you and your space.

7. Let the candles burn down completely. When they have fully extinguished, bury the coconut in your yard. If you do not have a yard, you may put the coconut in a box or leave it near a tree in a park.

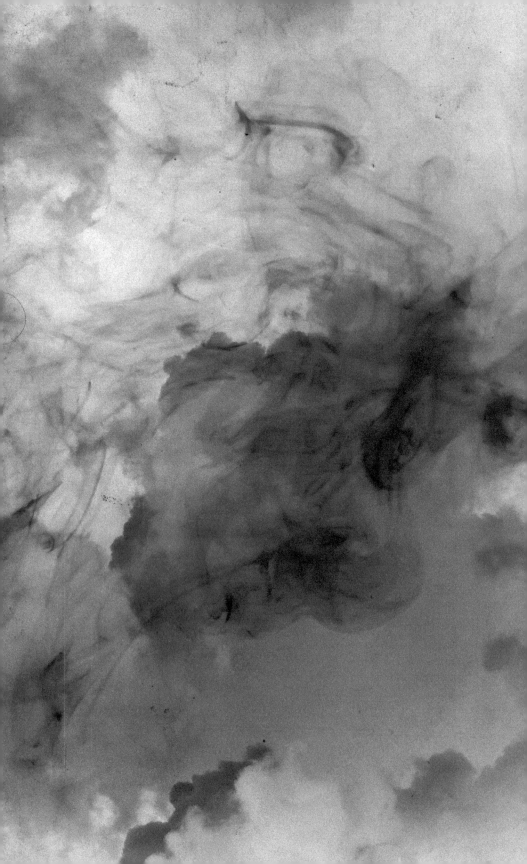

## CHAPTER NINE

# SPELLS FOR ABUNDANCE

Looking to generate additional income? Want to get that job promotion? In this chapter, you'll find spells geared toward abundance and prosperity, giving you access to some truly beneficial forms of money magic.

# Inviting Abundance, Achieving Prosperity

Spells for prosperity and abundance aren't just for gaining wealth or vast sums of money. They're intended to maintain financial stability, attract a bit of luck, and help you acquire career success. These spells won't make heaps of money materialize before your very eyes, but they will help push those doors open.

## Common Items Used for Abundance Spells

**Candles:** Figure, chime, tealight, votive, novena, pullout
**Colors:** Green, yellow, purple, black
**Herbs:** High John root, basil, cinnamon, rosemary, bay leaf
**Oils:** Patchouli, almond, vetiver, honeysuckle
**Crystals:** Citrine, pyrite, malachite, tiger's-eye, amber, garnet

# PUCK'S LUCKY COIN SPELL

This quick little spell calls upon Puck, the trickster fairy from English lore made famous in Shakespeare's *A Midsummer Night's Dream*. This spell can be done whenever you see any kind of coin turned heads up—a sign of good luck. Perform this spell on the same day you find the coin to maintain the connection and preserve the longevity of the luck.

## MAGICAL ITEMS REQUIRED

1 coin you found heads up (for luck)

Heatproof dish or plate

Matches or lighter

1 black or green chime candle (for prosperity and balance)

## PERFORMING THE SPELL

1. Take the coin that you found and hold it in both hands. Close your eyes and say, "I found a coin, it was heads up, now it's my charm to bring me luck."

2. Place the coin on the dish heads up. Using matches or a lighter, hold the flame to the bottom of the chime candle just long enough to melt a bit of the wax.

3. Place the chime candle on top of the coin. Let it cool, making sure that the candle wax has hardened and is now securely attached to the coin.

4. Once the candle has cooled and is securely placed on top of the coin, light the candle and say, "I light this candle, I call on Puck, please don't let anything disrupt my luck."

5. Let the candle burn down completely. When the candle has extinguished and the wax has melted over the coin, let the wax cool and keep the coin as a personal talisman for luck and prosperity.

6. Remember to thank Puck after your spell, as fairies can be resentful if not acknowledged or thanked for their assistance. Leave a small offering, such as a piece of cookie, bread, or apple slices, as a way of saying thank you.

# GET THAT JOB JINX

This abundance spell is used to find a job, get a promotion, and block those who may seek to compromise your success. With this spell, you will foil the plans of anyone who may wish to set you off course, such as co-workers who are up for the same promotion. It will also put you in the running for any potential new positions you might desire. Perform this spell on a Wednesday before an initial job interview.

## MAGICAL ITEMS REQUIRED

1 green novena or 7-day candle (for money)

3 drops frankincense oil

Images, items, and paperwork that represent the job in question
(you may write, type, or create an advertisement if you don't have anything else)

Pinch basil (for prosperity)

Pinch nutmeg (for luck)

Pinch clove (for security)

Pinch rosemary (for protection)

Matches or lighter

## PERFORMING THE SPELL

1. Hold the candle in both hands and charge it with your desire.

2. Dress the candle with frankincense oil, starting at the top and working toward the base.

3. Arrange the images that represent the desired job or work position. Place the candle on top of them.

4. Sprinkle the herbs on top of and around the candle in a circular motion. Meanwhile, sprinkle herbs onto the job-related images, too.

5. Light the candle, let it burn for an hour, then snuff or pinch it out with your fingers.

6. Continue this process at the same time for an hour every day until the candle has completely melted down and extinguished itself.

7. Take the wax and spell remnants, and bury them in your front yard, backyard, or in a potted plant.

8. After an initial interview or after vocalizing your desire for a job or different position, make sure to send a follow-up e-mail or make your interest known.

# MERCURY'S MANIFESTATION MAGIC

Mercury is the god of travelers, communication, luck, and gambling. He can be a wonderful asset to those who wish to achieve certain goals, especially when career, prosperity, or abundance are concerned. Perform this spell when you need help obtaining a certain desire or adding an extra bit of divine energy to what you're manifesting. This spell is best performed on a Monday and completed on a Wednesday, the day ruled by Mercury.

## MAGICAL ITEMS REQUIRED

Small carving tool

1 blue chime candle (for creativity)

3 chime candleholders

Matches or lighter

1 white chime candle (for divine influence)

1 green chime candle (for prosperity)

1 small piece of petition paper

## PERFORMING THE SPELL

1. Using the carving tool, carve the planetary symbol for Mercury onto one side of the blue chime candle, and your initials on the other side.

2. Hold the candle in your left hand and say, "Mercury in your flight, recognize my will and might, manifest my goal tonight." Place the chime candle in the candleholder.

3. Light the blue candle and let it burn down completely. Remember the time you started the spell, as you will begin again tomorrow at the same time.

4. Repeat step 1 on the following day, this time with the white chime candle.

5. Hold the white chime candle in your right hand and say, "I manifest what I desire; Mercury, hear me as I light this fire." Place the chime candle in the candleholder.

6. Light the white candle and let it burn down completely.

7. Repeat step 1 again on the following day with the green candle. Hold the green candle in both hands and say, "Mercury, hear my petition, let my spell come to fruition." Place the chime candle in the candleholder.

8. Light the candle and let it burn down completely.

9. Fold the petition paper into threes and place it under your bed for a full month.

# LUCKY CAT CANDLE

Figure candles are very popular among those who practice candle magic and are often used in folk magic, Hoodoo, Voodoo, Santería, and other spiritual traditions. This traditional Hoodoo spell is used to draw luck and money into your life, especially when you need it quickly. Cats have always been linked to the supernatural realm. Though a black cat is widely considered to be bad luck (especially if one crosses your path), they are actually considered good luck in British, Japanese, and Scottish folklore. Eighteenth-century pirates believed that black cats were omens of good luck and brought their super-stitions to the Caribbean and the Americas. Perform this spell on a Monday or Friday (or Friday the 13th if you'd like some extra juju).

## MAGICAL ITEMS REQUIRED

Small carving tool

1 black cat figure candle (for fast luck; a black 7-day candle will work as a substitute if needed)

3 drops patchouli oil

Pinch cinnamon (for prosperity)

Pinch crushed bay leaf (for luck)

Pinch nutmeg (for abundance)

Matches or lighter

Timer

White or black cloth or rag

## PERFORMING THE SPELL

1. Using the carving tool, carve your name and birthdate on the backside of the black cat figure candle.

2. Place 3 drops of patchouli oil on the head of the figure candle and apply it from the wick downward to the base of the candle. Meditate on your intentions during this process. What do you wish to achieve? How do you see your luck manifesting?

3. Sprinkle the candle with the cinnamon, bay leaf, and nutmeg.

4. Light the candle and pray for the manifestation of your intentions. You may speak your words aloud or internally.

5. Allow the candle to burn for 13 minutes—you may want to set a timer—before snuffing out the flame. (Don't blow it out.) Take note of what time you started the spell.

6. Repeat steps 4 and 5.

7. Repeat this process each night at the same time, until either the desire has been granted, or the candle has burned out entirely.

8. Place the candle wax and remnants in a piece of cloth and bury it near your front doorway.

# MAMAN BRIGITTE'S PROSPERITY SPELL

Prosperity allows you to feel secure and better help others as well as yourself. This spell enhances financial gain and attracts abundance. Maman Brigitte, the Vodou loa of death and fertility, has been known to assist those in need of change and good fortune. Consider using a black or purple cloth on your altar when you perform the spell, as those are sacred colors to Maman Brigitte. When performing this ritual, try to let the candle burn for an hour while meditating on your intent before snuffing out the candle. If you can, try to let the candle burn down completely, or continue the ritual for an hour every Monday until the candle has finished. (Monday is the best day to perform this spell because it is the day of the moon.) When the candle is gone, place the bowl on your altar and continue to use it as a prosperity bowl. The continued use of the prosperity bowl feeds the energy and magic and fuels the essence of the ritual.

## MAGICAL ITEMS REQUIRED

Cleansing herbs like frankincense, sweetgrass, or sage (optional)

Glass bowl

Salt

Green candle (novena, pillar, 7-day, or votive)

3 coins

Carving tool

Pinch rosemary (optional)

Matches or lighter

## PERFORMING THE SPELL

1. Concentrate on the part of your life where you wish to become more prosperous. Meditate on your desires and the missing components in your life that you may want to fill.

2. Close your eyes and take 3 deep breaths. Try to get to a relaxed state before performing the ritual.

3. Cleanse yourself and your space. (Cleansing is a great way to start any ritual.) Burn some frankincense, sweetgrass, or sage, and take a ritual bath or shower beforehand.

4. Fill a glass bowl with salt. Gather your candle, coins, and a carving tool as well as some rosemary if you have some.

5. Set the bowl of salt in front of your candle. Light the candle and ask Maman Brigitte to bless you with prosperity. Make sure that you speak your words and intentions aloud to your candle, even if it's in a whisper. Words have magic; that's why it's called "spelling"! Speak your spell into fruition.

6. Take a few deep breaths, relax, and meditate on the bowl of salt. Imagine the salt absorbing all the obstacles that stand in your way.

7. Using the carving tool, carve a "$" symbol on the green candle. If you have some, sprinkle a pinch of rosemary over the candle to attract abundance and wealth.

8. Place the candle in the bowl of salt and imagine a circle of white light surrounding the candle. This space is your circle of protection and ensures your spellwork is safe.

9. Take the 3 coins and hold them in your hands. Imagine these coins are seeds, and with every seed you plant, a new prosperous venture appears for you. Take the first coin and hold it to your forehead while closing your eyes. What do you wish to

see grow? What do you need more of in your life? Once you have thought about it, place the coin in the bowl of salt with the candle.

10. Repeat step 9 with the remaining coins. Once you have placed the third coin in the salt, place your hands over the bowl and candle, and close your eyes. Imagine the salt draining you of your fears and doubts. Imagine a fortress of protection surrounding your spellwork, your finances, and yourself. Focus on the coins and imagine those doubling in value.

11. Light the candle and let it burn for 1 or 2 hours. Imagine the candle attracting all aspects of prosperity and burning away all obstacles.

12. When the candle has burned down—or, if needed, been safely extinguished—continue to put additional coins such as pocket change into the bowl, to enhance the enchantment and feed the magic. Continue adding coins until the next full moon.

# 'EET, SWEET ABUNDANCE HONEY JAR

Honey jars, a staple in Southern conjure and Hoodoo, are meant to sweeten and entice the universe and people around you to give you the goods. Don't be afraid to think outside the box with this spell. What do you desire? Riches? Fame? No wish is too big for this spell. Just make sure you're specific with your intent—you might actually get what you wish for. This spell is best performed during the afternoon on a Saturday or Wednesday.

## MAGICAL ITEMS REQUIRED

Paper

Pen

1 mason jar

Honey (for influence and sweetness)

1 green votive or taper candle (for prosperity)

Matches or lighter

## PERFORMING THE SPELL

1. On a piece of paper, write a list of all your dreams and desires. What do you want more of?

2. Fill the mason jar halfway with honey. As you pour, think of the honey as abundance that you're filling the jar with. Continue to think of the things you wish to attract.

3. Tightly fold up the piece of paper 9 times and drop it into the jar of honey.

4. Take your finger, scoop up some of the honey, and put it in your mouth. Eat the honey and say, "Sweet abundance I desire, bring this spell to fruition with sacred fire."

5. Seal the jar and place the candle on top. (You may want to melt the bottom of the candle first to secure it to the lid.)

6. Light the candle. As the flame burns, say aloud a few of the wishes you put in your list. Close your eyes and imagine all that fulfills you.

7. Let the candle burn down completely.

8. Repeat steps 4 through 6 on a Saturday or Wednesday for the next 4 weeks. Let the candle wax melt and encase the honey jar.

9. When you have achieved some of the abundance you desired, open the jar and taste some of the honey, or use it to sweeten your tea.

10. You may continue to use the same jar and perform this spell again until you have received all the abundance you desire.

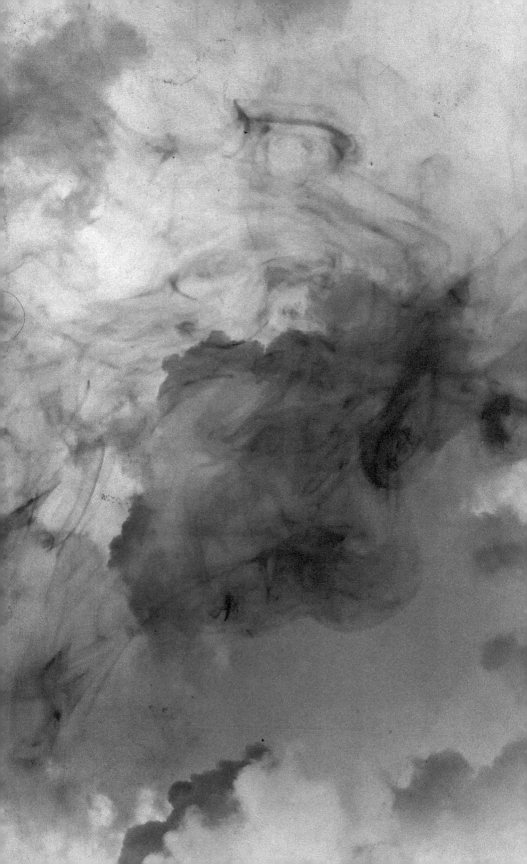

## CHAPTER TEN

# SPELLS FOR ENLIGHTENMENT

In this chapter, you will discover spells intended to boost your energy, contribute to happiness, and create a more positive environment in your personal life.

# Embracing Happiness, Experiencing Enlightenment

Sometimes, feeling sad, lonely, or depressed can take you to a very unpleasant place. These are all normal feelings that everyone has from time to time. The spells in this chapter will assist you when those feelings occur. Candle magic is a wonderful way to soothe feelings of anxiety and help promote positive and uplifting energies that can transform sorrow to hope and happiness.

## Common Items Used for Enlightenment Spells

**Colors:** Blue, yellow, orange, white
**Crystals:** Clear quartz, labradorite, onyx, citrine, carnelian, rose quartz
**Oils:** Bergamot, lavender, vetiver, frankincense
**Herbs:** St. John's wort, damiana, lavender, lemon balm, rose

# SUN & MOON HAPPINESS SPELL

When I was a teenager dealing with depression and anxiety, my mentor taught me this happiness spell that harnesses solar and lunar energy. Although it is a little time-consuming, the spell really did help pull me out of depression and balance my emotions. This multi-day candlelighting process is known as a vigil, and it is meant to keep you alert and pull you out of any negative space. Start this spell on a Sunday afternoon and continue it until the following Sunday, or until the candle extinguishes completely.

## MAGICAL ITEMS REQUIRED

1 orange or yellow novena candle (for the sun and solar energy)
1 white or black novena candle (for the moon and lunar energy)
Matches or lighter
Timer

## PERFORMING THE SPELL

1. Place the candles that represent the sun and the moon on a table in your room, or wherever you can have privacy to conduct your spellwork.

2. Starting on a Sunday afternoon, hold the sun candle in both your hands and say, "Spirit of the sun, you of many names, when I light this candle please come through in the flames. Ra, Mithras, Apollo, Sol, Lugh, these are only a few names for you. Brighten my days, protect me with your light. Help fight my fears before blending tonight."

3. Light the sun candle and let it burn for 30 minutes. Look at the flame and imagine the flame as a person or spirit dancing

in the candle. What shapes do you see? What forms does the flame take on? When the time has ended, snuff out the candle with your fingers or using a tool. (Don't blow out the candle.)

4. After a few hours, when it's become evening or before you go to bed, hold the moon candle in both your hands and say, "Spirit of the moon, you of many names, when I light this candle please come through in the flames. Isis, Diana, Artemis, Hecate, Selene, your names are many, your powers supreme. Protect me with your light in the darkest of night, and when I feel sorrow cast it out of sight. As I light this flame, let your magic burn bright."

5. Light the moon candle and let it burn for 30 minutes. Visualize your fears and sorrows being cast out of your body. Imagine any darkness, anger, or negativity being blasted out by a white light.

6. Continue lighting the sun candle during the day and the moon candle in the evening. If you don't have 30 minutes to devote to the process each day, you can instead light the candles for 13 minutes (13 is a magical number). Always remember to snuff out the candles to extinguish them—never blow them out.

7. When the candles have completely extinguished, thank the spirits of the sun and moon, and recycle the candle glasses to keep the vibrations of the spell working.

# ST. EXPEDITE QUICK FIX CANDLE

Yes, you read that right—St. Expedite is the patron saint of speedy cases. Whatever the obstacle—court cases, legal issues, business problems, conflict in relationships, or finishing an exam or task—St. Expedite is definitely worth petitioning. Call on him when you need a solution or when time is of the essence. I learned this simple New Orleans spell during my time in the French Quarter and have used it countless times. You may make an altar for St. Expedite with red cloth and gold or silver accents or candleholders. Perform this spell on a Wednesday, or any day in the afternoon.

## MAGICAL ITEMS REQUIRED

3 drops cinnamon oil (for time/urgency)

Red novena candle (St. Expedite's sacred color)

Red marker

1 small piece of paper

Matches or lighter

Flowers (for blessings)

Bowl of water

Pound cake (for an offering)

## PERFORMING THE SPELL

1. Pour 3 drops of cinnamon oil on top of the red novena candle to heat the spell up. Hold the candle in both hands, imagine the scenario at hand, and visualize it being resolved with the utmost urgency.

2. Using the red marker, write your petition on a small piece of paper and place it under the candle.

3.  Place both hands over the candle and say, "St. Expedite, please come my way, hear me and what I have to say, grant my petition, don't waste another day."

4.  Light the candle and let it burn completely.

5.  Recite the prayer once a day until your petition has been answered.

6.  Once the candle has burned down completely, place some flowers in a bowl of water next to the burned-out candle, and a small piece of pound cake on a plate on the other side of the candle. If you do not make these offerings to St. Expedite, it is said that he will take back your request and then some.

7.  Sit at the table or altar you've prepared and indulge in a piece of pound cake for yourself.

8.  When you've finished the spell, recycle the candle glass and place the piece of pound cake under a tree, or sprinkle the cake on the ground for the birds.

# A VERY MERRY UNBIRTHDAY WISH SPELL

*There are 364 days when you might get un-birthday presents, and only one for birthday presents, you know.*

—*Lewis Carroll,* Alice's Adventures in Wonderland

Guess what? Chances are that you've technically performed candle magic before, even if you've never practiced witch-craft or magic until now. Have you ever made a wish on your birthday before blowing out a candle? That's candle magic! Who says you have to wait for your birthday to make magic? Perform this spell whenever you want to make a wish. Despite the birthday tradition of blowing out the candle, be sure to snuff out the candle's flame with your fingers instead.

If you're wondering about how to choose what to wish for, remember that a wish requires less energy than an intention; therefore, the rule of thumb would be that anything you wish for isn't necessarily a must-have in your life. Trivial things, or a luxury, are good candidates for a wish.

## MAGICAL ITEMS REQUIRED
1 piece of cake or cupcake (for happiness)
1 birthday candle (for wish fulfillment)

Matches or lighter

## PERFORMING THE SPELL

1. Place the candle in the cake or cupcake and conjure up feelings of happiness. Imagine it is your birthday, or a time of celebration.

2. Choose your wish. Imagine it intently in your mind.

3. Light the candle.

4. Close your eyes and envision your wish being granted.

5. Open your eyes and snuff the candle out between your fingers.

6. Eat the cake and enjoy.

7. Keep the candle under your bed until your actual birthday, and then bury it in the yard.

# CIRCE'S SELF-TRANSFORMATION SPELL

Sometimes you need to get out of your skin and be seen as someone else. This spell is crafted for times when you are pulled to a new path, spiritual journey, friend group, or personal style. Circe, a demi-goddess in Greek mythology and one of the first witches of antiquity, is best known from *The Odyssey;* in it, she transformed Odysseus's men into pigs. She is renowned for her vast knowledge of potions, charms, and herbs, which she used to manifest, manipulate, and transform things at her will. Tap into the powers of Circe when it's time to switch things up. This spell should be performed on a Monday or during a full moon.

## MAGICAL ITEMS REQUIRED

1 black votive candle (for transformation)

1 purple votive candle (for magic)

Heatproof dish

Matches or lighter

Pinch rosemary (for protection)

Pinch lavender (for attraction)

Pinch crushed bay leaf (for prosperity)

1 drop dragon's blood oil (for alchemy/transformation)

## PERFORMING THE SPELL

1. Place both candles on a heatproof dish.

2. Take the black candle in both hands and visualize how you'd like to be perceived; imagine the clothing you'd want to wear, and the changes you'd like to see in your life. When you've finished with this visualization, place the candle back on the dish.

3. Hold the purple votive in both your hands and say, "Divine Circe, hear my plea, assist in my magic and transform me, let them see what I wish to be."

4. Light the purple votive and tip it over the black candle, letting the melted wax drip onto it. Let the wax drip for a while, being careful not to burn yourself.

5. Return the lit purple candle to the dish and sprinkle the rosemary, lavender, and bay leaf over the black candle.

6. Place a drop of dragon's blood oil on the black candle and light it.

7. Let both candles burn down completely. Watch as the candles melt and fuse together, and how the herbs and oil blend and transform. As the candles melt, visualize that you yourself are also being transformed.

8. When the candles have burned down completely and extinguished, bury their remnants in the yard or in a potted plant.

# INNER GOD/DESS DIVINE SPELL

Everyone has a little divine energy—you just have to learn how to tap into it. This spell is great for manifesting strength and courage. Perform this spell when you need a little recognition from others or want to be noticed and appreciated. This spell is best done on a Sunday.

## MAGICAL ITEMS REQUIRED

1 white chime candle (for divinity)

Chime candleholder

Matches or lighter

1 drop vetiver oil (for happiness)

Carnelian stone (for strength)

## PERFORMING THE SPELL

1. Hold the white chime candle in your dominant hand, close your eyes, and say, "I am sacred, I'm divine, I reclaim what's rightfully mine."

2. Place the candle in the holder and light it.

3. While the candle is burning, place a drop of vetiver oil into the palm of your dominant hand and anoint the carnelian stone.

4. Clutch the stone in your hand, close your eyes, and say, "As this candle burns with sacred fire, unleash in me the divine, they all desire."

5. Place the stone next to the candle and continue to let the candle burn.

6. When the candle has burned down completely, reclaim the carnelian stone and keep it with you whenever you need strength or courage, or you wish to be seen.

# DRUID'S CIRCLE OF SERENITY

Whenever anxiety or stress takes over, I turn to this ritual. It is a nice complement to meditation and can also be used in combination with other spells. The druids, ancient shamans and keepers of magic in the Celtic world, knew how to connect with nature, spirits, and their higher selves. Most of all, they knew the importance of serenity. This ritual should be done during the evening starting on an even-numbered hour (e.g., 8 p.m., 10 p.m.). You may use additional candles if desired, but try to remain consistent with their size and shape. If you'd like a bigger circle, use more candles on an extra-sturdy holder. You may play music that soothes you and bring any crystals or tools you wish to charge.

## MAGICAL ITEMS REQUIRED

6 candles of any style, preferably tealights or votives

Matches or lighter

Incense (preferably frankincense, myrrh, or lavender)

Incense holder

Soothing music (optional)

## PERFORMING THE SPELL

1. Arrange the candles in a circle around you. Be sure to give yourself enough room to move around so you don't knock any over. Place one candle directly in front of you, one behind you, one to your left, one to your right, and so forth.

2. After you've finished arranging the candles, light the incense and slowly turn clockwise, waving the incense around. Imagine clearing out this circle and creating a sacred space. Continue this process until you've made a complete circle.

3. Place the incense in the holder directly in front of you. Kneel for a moment and envision a circle of white light surrounding you. Watch as the incense smoke forms a mist.

4. Starting in front of you, begin lighting all the candles in a clockwise motion, imagining the circle getting stronger as you light each one.

5. Once all the candles have been lit, find a comfortable sitting position. You may play music at this time if you wish. Stare at the flames around you and imagine a barrier protecting you from the outside world. Imagine the flames attracting the positive spirits and energies, and fueling your magic and spirituality. In this circle, anything is possible. Notice the incense smoke swirling around you.

6. Close your eyes and breathe. Imagine all your fears burning away in the flames. This space is your sacred circle of power. This space is where you will find serenity. This space is where you'll find the answers.

7. Stay in the circle as long as you like. Since there is no set intention on the candles, you may blow them out when you are finished.

8. If you have not finished the candles off, keep them as your designated circle candles to use whenever you want to harness the druids' power of serenity.

# LET THE FLAME BURN BRIGHT

Now that the candle has been extinguished and the spellwork is in motion, take a moment to reflect on what you've learned in this book. In addition to learning about candle magic, you've learned about self-transformation, the power of intent, and the fire that dwells not only in the flames but also within yourself. You should feel proud and congratulate yourself for taking this journey into the world of magic!

I hope you will continue to follow the path to candle magic. When you look at a candle henceforth you will no longer see a mundane object, but a true source of power. You will know the history of magic contained within that candle, and how to utilize its energy to serve your desired purpose. Don't put *all* your stock in the candle, though, as it is important to remember that the magic lives with you.

Before we part ways, allow me to share a few more tips that will help you grow and deepen your practice:

- Do not rush your rituals or spellwork, even if you feel that you only have a limited amount of time or privacy. Instead, wait until you can give the work your full attention.

- Don't forget to look at the wax when the candle is done burning. What shapes do you see? Was it a clean or messy burn? Use your intuition to gauge what the melted wax means about the outcome of the spell.

- Keep a journal or diary to write down and keep track of your spells. Note how the spells turned out, and if you used any substitutions or tried anything different from what was instructed.

- Wax can be used for talismans and amulets, so pocket some if you want to keep the energy of the spell close to you, especially if the wax makes a circular or symbolic shape. Candle wax divination is known as ceromancy and can add a rich complexity to your candle magic.

- Pay attention to the way the candle burns to learn how the spirits and universe will communicate with you.

- If you decide to incorporate spirits or deities in your working, always be respectful. Remember to leave offerings before the spell, and always give thanks afterward. Working with spirit guides, ancestors, and deities should feel balanced, so be careful not to make demands or try to control these forces or energies.

- Research different mythologies, folklore, and pantheons to see what calls to you. If there is a spirit or deity mentioned in a spell that you do not connect with, find another one with similar traits. Look at your own cultural ties and see if there's a family folk spirit you can connect with. And know that you don't have to include a spirit or deity if you don't feel comfortable working with one.

- The sulfur in matches contains protective energy, so keep a discarded match close to the candle after you've used it to dispel outside forces affecting your magic.

- Take pride in your work when you carve your candle. After you anoint it with oil, you may want to add glitter to it and rub it in the carved design. Many practitioners use glitter to add a little more oomph to their working, especially when it's for another person.

I encourage you to continue following the path of candle magic by exploring other ways of incorporating the element of fire in your spellwork. Whether it be lamps, scrying, or kitchen magic, the spirit of fire is on your side and ready to assist you. Research different aspects of magic, spirituality, and the occult. Expand your knowledge of herblore, crystals, oils, and folklore. Experiment with adapting these spells to better assist your needs, and don't be afraid to substitute one herb or oil for another if you have a preference. Once you've done enough research and feel comfortable with ritual and spellwork, you will find that performing magic becomes second nature. The herbs will call to you, the spell required will flow through you, and the process will get easier as you become more attuned to the elements you're working with.

And remember, regardless of the situation or obstacle, there's a candle for that! (#theresacandleforthat)

# TABLES OF CORRESPONDENCE

## Candle Colors

| BLACK | wisdom, death, renewal, resurrection |
|---|---|
| BLUE | peace, tranquility |
| BROWN | the earth, strength, balance, justice, earth magic, animal and pet spells, nature spirits |
| GOLD | abundance, prosperity, attraction, money |
| GRAY | knowledge, communication, spirit communication, neutralizing negative energy, wisdom |
| GREEN | luck, prosperity, wealth, fertility, stability, abundance, success |
| INDIGO | renewal, relaxation, reflection, new beginnings |
| ORANGE | energy, exuberance, courage, the sun, positive outcomes, job successes, wish fulfillment |
| PINK | affection, compassion, beauty, fidelity, new love, happiness, romantic relationships, monogamy, marriage |
| PURPLE | royalty, the divine, power, the supernatural |
| RED | life force, vitality, attraction, sensuality, desire, ambition, virility, strength, birth, death, achieving goals, overcoming obstacles, love |
| SILVER | clairvoyance, motherhood, marriage, psychic work, money, financial stability, peace |
| WHITE | life, fertility, nourishment, goodness, balance, death, structure |
| YELLOW | brilliance, joy, clarity, insight, clairvoyance, unhexing, uncrossing, protection, guidance |

## Herbs

| | |
|---|---|
| ALLSPICE | healing, luck, business attraction, money, prosperity |
| ANGELICA ROOT | joy, happiness, empowerment, spiritual communication, protection, healing |
| ANISE | psychic development, protection from the evil eye, spirit communication |
| BASIL | happiness, money, confidence, love, protection |
| BAY LAUREL | wishing, success, healing, psychic visions, cleansing, wisdom, power |
| CATNIP | love, sexuality, peace, protection of children |
| CINNAMON | money, protection, energy boost, spirituality boost, success, libido |
| CLOVES | money, luck, friendship |
| DAMIANA | love, sex, aphrodisiac, lust, passion, romance, attraction |
| JASMINE | moon magic, love, feminine energy, spirituality, peace, money, sexuality, health |
| LAVENDER | protection, sleep, happiness, peace, astral projection, meditation, love, purification |
| LEMONGRASS | purification, road opener, home in earth, spirit work, cleansing |
| MUGWORT | psychic powers, prophetic dreams, astral projection, protection, spirit work, strength, deity work, necromancy, divination |
| NUTMEG | luck, energy boost, money, raise vibrations, increase psychic awareness |
| PEPPER (BLACK/WHITE) | protection, return to sender, grounding, hex breaker |
| ROSE | love, peace, sex, romance, beauty, self-esteem |
| ROSEMARY | protection, cleansing, love, longevity, health, magic boost |
| SAGE | calming, longevity, wisdom, relaxation, inspiration, spiritual cleansing, fumigation |
| THYME | luck, dreams, money, financial stability, peace |

| VALERIAN ROOT | love, purification, marriage, return to sender, ritual purification, love, sleep |
|---|---|
| VERVAIN | protection, aphrodisiac, inspiration, protection, hex breaker, spirit protection |
| WORMWOOD | prophecy, psychic development, healing, creativity, love, peace, wisdom, ancestral magic |
| YARROW | love, psychic enhancement, wisdom, courage, depression, mental health, clarity |

# Oils

| | |
|---|---|
| AMBER | money, sensuality, goddess energy, psychic, ancestral work, protection |
| BERGAMOT | money, happiness, cleansing, peace |
| CYPRESS | healing, comfort, grieving, longevity |
| DRAGON'S BLOOD | magic, power, protection, healing, luck, spiritual clearing |
| EUCALYPTUS | healing, protection, uncrossing |
| FRANKINCENSE | protection, purification, spirituality, meditation, anxiety, fear, soothing, calmness, higher consciousness |
| HONEYSUCKLE | prosperity, psychic awareness, protection, sweetness of life, spiritual insight, goal fulfillment |
| JASMINE | confidence, love, sex, money, peace, spirituality, insight, lunar magic |
| LOTUS | Egyptian magic, wisdom, blessings, goddess magic |
| MUSK | courage, masculine energy, fertility, attraction, lust, sex magic |
| MYRRH | protection, purification, meditation, grounding, confidence, spiritual awakening, spiritual fumigation |
| OLIVE OIL | purification, cleansing, divine energy, spiritual awakening, spirit work, ritual purification |
| ORANGE BLOSSOM | joy, money, happiness, personal development, banish negative thoughts |
| PATCHOULI | fertility, physical energy, romance, partnership, divine self, attraction, money |
| PEPPERMINT | protection, calming, wisdom, spirituality, cleansing, happiness, positivity stimulant |
| ROSE | beauty, love, sex, peace, psychic protection, honesty |
| SANDALWOOD | wish fulfillment, healing, spirituality, protection, sexual awakening, attraction, higher consciousness |
| VANILLA | love, magic, mental awareness, energy, sex, fights depression, relationships |
| VIOLET | love, wish fulfillment, healing, calmness, peace |
| YLANG-YLANG | aphrodisiac, attraction, euphoria, relaxation, bliss, love, grounding |

# Days of the Week

| SUNDAY | "Suns day" is a time to perform spells for manifestation, male energy, divine power, courage, spells for happiness, success, and job opportunities. |
|---|---|
| MONDAY | "Moons day" is ruled by the power of the moon. On this day perform spells for lunar deities, dreamwork, spiritual growth, psychic and divination work, healing, and cleansing. |
| TUESDAY | "Mars day" is ruled by Mars, the planet named after the Roman god of war. This day is good for performing spells for courage, conflict resolution, virility, and gaining wisdom or overcoming obstacles. |
| WEDNESDAY | "Mercury's day" is ruled by the planet Mercury. This day is the perfect time for spellwork involving self-improvement, communication, divination, travel, friendships, and spirit communication. |
| THURSDAY | Ruled by the planet Jupiter, this day is great for spells regarding money, legal matters, luck, and success. |
| FRIDAY | Ruled by the planet Venus and the Norse fertility goddess Frigg, this day is for special work and rituals concerning love, friendship, art, creativity, pleasure, and fertility. |
| SATURDAY | Ruled by the planet Saturn, this day is great for spellwork and rituals concerning banishing, hex breaking, cleansing, healing, return to sender, and motivation. |

## Lunar Cycles

| NEW MOON | new beginnings, uncover hidden agendas, uncover the truth, spiritual awakening, cleansing, protection of home and self, bindings |
|----------|---------------------------------------------------------------------------------------------------------------------------------|
| WAXING MOON | money spells, financial stability, job attraction, energy intensity, abundance, growth |
| FULL MOON | healing, wish fulfillment, goddess magic, prosperity, spirit work, love magic, attraction |
| WANING MOON | banishing, purge, getting rid of negativity, protection, change, letting go |

## Stones

| AGATE | health, luck, gambling |
|---|---|
| AMBER | love, luck, transformation |
| AMETHYST | fights addiction, psychic awareness, insight, healing, crown chakra, spirit work |
| APACHE TEARS | protection, comfort, ancestral magic, cleansing |
| BLOODSTONE | stone of courage, purification, clearing negativity, balance |
| CARNELIAN | creation, creativity, life force, fear, stability, virility, health |
| CITRINE | prosperity, abundance, money, mental focus, endurance |
| HEMATITE | health, grounding, return to sender, relaxation, peace, spirit work |
| JASPER | protection, mental clarity |
| JET | protection, earth magic, spirit cleanse, manifestation enhancement |
| LAPIS LAZULI | divine energy, protection, health |
| MOONSTONE | lunar magic, balance, reflection, new beginnings, creative energies, increase intuition and insight |
| OBSIDIAN | protection, hex breaker, grounding, spirit work |
| TIGER'S-EYE | grounding, creativity, wisdom, insight, emotional balance, raises vibrations |

# RESOURCES

## Books

**The Element Encyclopedia of Secret Signs and Symbols** by
**Adele Nozedar**
A great resource for looking up symbols you may see in wax, dreams, clouds, etc.

**Encyclopedia of Witchcraft** by **Judika Illes**
This book is a must-have for all practitioners as well as those interested in learning more about witchcraft. Whether you're looking for information on a deity, tool, specific practice, or history, this book is your go-to reference guide.

**The Master Book of Herbalism** by **Paul Beyerl**
Probably the best book on herbs available for a magical practitioner, this book contains in-depth information about herb lore, oils, incense, elixirs, and uses for magic.

**Voodoo Hoodoo Spellbook** by **Denise Alvarado**
This book is a wonderful resource filled with history, authentic spells, recipes, and more—all focusing on the Voodoo of New Orleans.

# Podcasts

### Bigfoot Collectors Club

A paranormal podcast hosted by Michael McMillian and Bryce Johnson that explores ghost sightings, folklore, historical anomalies, the occult, and high strangeness.

@bigfootcollectorsclub

### The Witch and The Medium

I co-host this podcast with my friend and famed medium Adela Lavigne. Each week, we talk about our different practices, gifts, and beliefs, and share our experiences with the supernatural and knowledge on different topics.

@thewitchandthemedium

TheWitchAndTheMedium.com

# Supplies

### Pan's Apothika (aka Panpipes)

This place is the first metaphysical shop I ever went to as a child. It carries hundreds of herbs and oils, and can custom prepare tools of intention. Vicky, the shop owner and a dear friend, specializes in individually anointed glass-enclosed candles, typically the 7-day kind, which is an excellent tool for manifesting one's intentions.

PanPipes.com

(323) 891-5936

### III Crows Crossroads

Charmed essentials for everyone! I started this company with two of my fellow coven members. The shop blends together the magic of traditional witchcraft, Voodoo, Santería, and American folk conjure. You'll find soaps, candles, oils, spell kits, and many more enchanting items to get you started on your spiritual journey.

@3crowscrossroads

Etsy.com/shop/IIICrowsCrossroads

**The Olde World Emporium**

The Olde World Emporium, co-owned by Mystic Dylan, is Santa Clarita's premier metaphysical shop. The shop carries herbs, oils, books, crystals, candles, and classes.

23127 Lyons Avenue

Newhall, CA 91321

661-666-7507

www.OldeWorldEmporium.com

Instagram: @TheOldeWorldEmporium

Facebook: facebook.com/TheOldeWorldEmporium

Twitter: @olde_world

# YouTube

**The Witch of Wonderlust**

Led by my friend Olivia, this YouTube channel is a great resource for videos that feature how-to's and tutorials for beginner witches as well as a tutorial on candle magic with yours truly that inspired the hashtag #theresacandleforthat.

YouTube.com/user/TossingSpades

# GLOSSARY

You may find that not all of these words are used in the book; however, they appear here to increase your understanding of candle magic.

ALTAR: A table or secret space that is used for ritual, sacrifices, offerings, or spellwork.

AMULET: An ornament or charm that is used to give protection against evil danger or disease.

ANOINT: To dress a candle with oils.

CAPNOMANCY: Ancient divination method in which smoke from a burning fire (usually herbs, wood, or sacrifices) reveals omens.

CONJURE: A type of American folk magic that incorporates African, Native American, Jewish, Catholic, Christian, and European traditions.

CONSECRATE: To make something sacred, typically a tool that will be used for spiritual or magical purposes.

DEITY: A god, goddess, or divine spirit.

DIVINATION: The practice of seeking knowledge of the future or unknown through the use of tools or supernatural means.

HEX: To cast a spell or bewitch; commonly used for ill will, revenge, or with malicious intent.

JINX: Bad luck caused magically by another person, or through breaking a superstition or folk belief.

JUJU: Objects such as amulets, spells, and talismans that are used in religious practices. This practice derives from West Africa, and the term has been applied to traditional African religions and folk practices.

LIBANOMANCY: Divination through observing incense smoke.

MAGIC: The ability to subdue or manipulate energies, both natural and supernatural.

NOVENA: From the Latin word meaning "nine," a traditional style of devotional praying in Christianity and Catholicism.

OMEN: A sign or event that is regarded with prophetic significance, which can be either good or bad.

PURIFICATION: To cleanse both spiritually and physically.

PYRE: A heap, or structure, that's usually made of wood and constructed to burn a body for a funeral ceremony.

PYROMANCY: Divination through the use of fire.

RITUAL: A sequence of activities that may involve gestures, words, or actions that are performed for spiritual enlightenment, or to gain magical momentum and tradition.

SCRYING: To gaze at various forms and surfaces that offer guidance, prophecy, and answers to potential questions through symbols and images that appear.

SEX MAGIC: Any type of sexual activity used for magical, ritualistic, or spiritual purposes. Sex magic often incorporates sexual arousal with visualization of a desired result that is powered energetically and spiritually through orgasm.

SIGIL: An inscribed or painted symbol that has magical power.

SNUFF: To put out a flame.

TALISMAN: An object, inscribed or handmade, that harnesses magical powers and energy.

VEVE: Specific spiritual symbols associated with the different loas and spirits of Voodoo.

VIGIL: A time of devotional watching or observance. In magic, the term typically refers to a multi-day spell or ritual that may last several hours or days.

# INDEX

# ACKNOWLEDGMENTS

I'm so grateful, and feel so blessed, to be able to present this book to you.

First, I'd like to thank Ashley Popp, Sean Newcott, and Rockridge Press for giving me the opportunity to craft and create this book.

I'd love to thank my parents, Steven and Ingrid, and my grandmother, Mom-Cat (aka Lillian), who let me be the wild imaginative child that I was, and didn't try to restrict me or influence me when I became interested in learning more about witchcraft, magic, and the occult.

To my brother, whose kindness and genuine support always inspires me.

To Vicky Adams of Pan's Apothika (aka Panpipes), who didn't bat an eye at the intrigued nine-year-old who walked into her shop and offered me my first safe haven.

To Kelly Spangler, who gave me a reading in Salem, Massachusetts, on my birthday and told me she saw me becoming a professional witch without me even saying a word.

To my sophomore English teacher, Shaneequa Cannon, whose teachings and friendship inspire me to this day.

To Lana, Leah, and Brenna, who not only took me in as their kin, but also fueled my desires and interests in candle magic.

To my Crows, Cyndi & Jess, who help me make magic every day.

To my coven for their support and community. And to Adela, who constantly keeps me in check.

To Nyt Myst, Bloody Mary, Laurie Johnson, and the many other magical mentors and teachers I have had, and, of course, my ancestors and spirits—thank you.

# ABOUT THE AUTHOR

 For more than two decades, **Mystic Dylan** has studied and perfected his craft in the occult. At age nine, Dylan and his mother frequented a local occult shop, where he became attracted to witchcraft. He mastered palmistry and tarot and eventually pursued a formal education in the occult arts. His natural connection to mysticism fueled his ongoing study and exploration of witchcraft, Voodoo, conjure, and shamanism. Now a professional witch, Dylan uses the craft to assist both friends and clients in their personal lives.

Born with Cuban, Irish, German, and Native American blood, he attributes his spiritual gifts to his many ancestors who walk and work beside him, guiding him on his sacred journey. An independent scholar and film and academic consultant, Mystic Dylan lives and works in Los Angeles, California, where he teaches classes, runs his own coven, and co-hosts *The Witch and The Medium* podcast. He co-owns the III Crows Crossroads online store and is the co-founder of the brick and mortar shop, The Olde World Emporium.